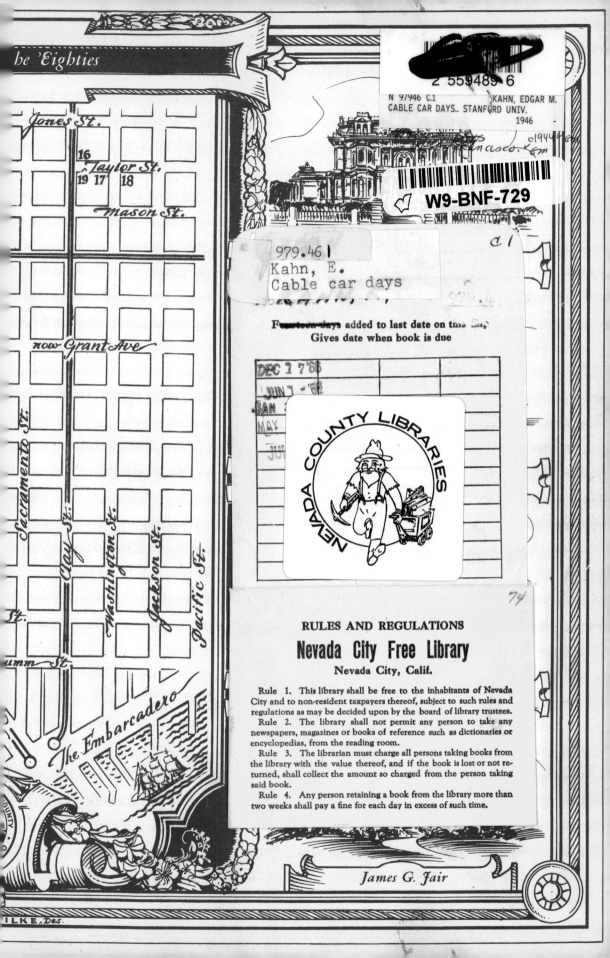

Jones St.

16
19 17 18
Taylor St.

Mason St.

now Grant Ave.

Sacramento St.

Clay St.

Washington St.

Jackson St.

Pacific St.

mm St.

The Embarcadero

74

RULES AND REGULATIONS
Nevada City Free Library
Nevada City, Calif.

James G. Fair

WILKE, Des.

CABLE CAR DAYS

In San Francisco

Cable Cars—A San Francisco Tradition

CABLE CAR DAYS

In San Francisco

By

EDGAR M. KAHN

STANFORD UNIVERSITY PRESS
STANFORD UNIVERSITY, CALIFORNIA

STANFORD UNIVERSITY PRESS, STANFORD UNIVERSITY, CALIFORNIA

THE BAKER AND TAYLOR COMPANY, 55 FIFTH AVE., NEW YORK 3, N.Y.
HENRY M. SNYDER & CO., 440 FOURTH AVE., NEW YORK 16, N.Y.

Copyright 1940 and 1944 by the Board of Trustees of the Leland Stanford Junior University
Printed and Bound in the United States of America by Stanford University Press

First edition, November 1940
Second printing, December 1940
Third printing, December 1940
Fourth printing, February 1941
Revised edition, October 1944
Sixth printing, January 1945
Seventh printing, November 1945
Eighth printing, January 1946

To my wife

ANNE

The Ballad
of the Hyde Street Grip

By GELETT BURGESS

[The ballad of old San Francisco was written by Gelett Burgess and published in 1901 in a volume of his verse *A Gage of Youth*. It is reprinted with his permission.]

Oh, the rain is slanting sharply, and the Norther's blowing cold;
When the cable strands are loosened she is nasty hard to hold!
There's little time for sitting down, and little chance for gab,
For the bumper guards the crossing, and you'd best be keeping tab,
Two-and-twenty "let-go's" every double trip—
It takes a bit of doing, on the Hyde Street Grip!

Throw her off at Powell Street, let her go at Post,
Watch her well at Geary and at Sutter when you coast!
Easy at the Power House, have a care at Clay,
Sacramento, Washington, Jackson—all the way!
Drop your rope at Union—never make a slip—
The lever keeps you busy, on the Hyde Street Grip!

Foot-brake, wheel-brake, slot-brake and gong,
You'd better keep 'em busy or you'll soon be going wrong!
Rush her on the crossings, catch her on the rise,
Easy round the corners when the dust is in your eyes—
And the bell will always stop you if you hit her up a clip;
You are apt to earn your wages on the Hyde Street Grip!

North Beach to Tenderloin, over Russian Hill,
The grades are something giddy, and the curves are fit to kill!
All the way to Market Street, climbing up the slope,
Down upon the other side, hanging to the rope!
But the view of San Francisco, as you take the lurching dip!
There is plenty of excitement on the Hyde Street Grip!

If you had to drive a penny bus from Chelsea to the Strand
You'd see Westminster Abbey, and you'd say that it was grand!
If you had to pass the Luxembourg and Place de la Concorde
Atop a Paris omnibus, no doubt you'd thank the Lord!
But the Frenchy'd give his chapeau and the Cockney'd give his whip
For a sight of San Francisco from the Hyde Street Grip!

Oh, the lights are in the Mission, and the ships are on the Bay,
And Tamalpais is looming from the Gate, across the way;
The Presidio trees are waving, and the hills are growing brown,
And the driving fog is harried from the ocean to the town!
How the pulleys slap and rattle! How the cables hum and skip!
Oh, they sing a gallant chorus to the Hyde Street Grip!

When the Orpheum is closing and the crowds are on the way,
The conductor's punch is ringing and the dummy's light and gay;
But the wait upon the switch above the beach is dark and still—
Just the swashing of the surges on the shore below the Mill;
And the Flash from Angel Island breaks across the Channel rip
As the hush of midnight falls upon the Hyde Street Grip!

FOREWORD

FOR MORE THAN half a century the cable cars of San Francisco have constituted one of the town's most characteristic features. There were cable cars in many other cities, but none which mount more picturesquely to the heights. Here, where this form of transportation originated, it still possesses a distinctive charm—the charm so delightfully immortalized by Gelett Burgess in "The Ballad of the Hyde Street Grip," which no San Franciscan ever completely forgets, no matter how far he may roam from the city of hills beside the Golden Gate.

It is therefore fitting that the story of the cable car be written and that it be written by a San Franciscan, one whose family background and business association has bound him closely to these hills and to the now quaint cars so inseparably a part of the landscape of San Francisco.

" 'Out for the curve!" How frequently the warning gripman's shout and his tiny vehicle's clanging bell have helped us greet the day! Mounting through wind and hurrying fog, crawling up over the steepest grades, their passengers clinging precariously to their sides, these little cars form a link with the past that will be keenly missed when time and economic change drive them for the last time to the shelter of the barn. Nor is that day far away, as the author here clearly indicates. Indeed, except for the California Street Cable Railroad Company, all the numerous cable enterprises have had their identities changed in various ways, or have passed out of existence.

This is an informal narrative rather than a technical monograph. Through its pages march many notable characters of the city's eventful past, and many a long-forgotten anecdote has here been recalled. Mr. Kahn's researches have disclosed numerous features of the cable-car story that might otherwise have been lost—as most of the actual records have disappeared or were destroyed when fire supervened the earthquake in 1906. Much of what follows came from the mouths of those who themselves or whose fathers were a part of the picture during the formative years of the city; and it is well that their tales be written down now, before the story in all its variety and flavor is forgotten.

"Cable Car Days"—the very phrase recalls tall hats and crinolines, the Comstock excitements and the coming of the Pacific Railroad, the nabobs of Nob Hill headed by "The Big Four" and their satellites, Kearney and his mob and their war cry, "The Chinese must go!" Those days have passed long years ago; but still the little cars go clanging up and down the hills of San Francisco, living relics of an earlier and braver day in the city that still sits upon its hills, "Serene, indifferent of Fate."

" 'Out for the curve!"

CARL I. WHEAT

SAN FRANCISCO, CALIFORNIA
October 1, 1940

PREFACE

THE ILLUSTRATIONS were executed by William Wilke, an artist who stands high in San Francisco. Genius such as his has contributed to the lofty position pen-and-ink work holds in the field of art.

I am thankful to Samuel I. Wormser, who gave me his recollections of events which took place when his father was the first treasurer of the California Street Cable Railroad Company.

Samuel Pond I thank for a copy of *Vignettes of Early San Francisco Homes and Gardens* and a considerable amount of helpful information regarding Nob Hill in the late 'eighties.

I am indebted to the late James W. Harris for his readiness to reconstruct for me the sixty-year history of the California Street Cable Railroad Company.

I desire to express my gratitude to the following: Lester Wells, Secretary of the Company, who assisted me in delving into records of directors' and stockholders' meetings dating back many years; Antoine Borel, Jr., George Coleman, S. Waldo Coleman, Harry Stetson, the late Ralph Hare, and Frank Buck, who provided me with information concerning their fathers' activities in the Company; Archie Treat, the late Joseph Cummings, David Oliver, and John McGaw, who contributed recollections of personalities; Fred Boeken, for the loan of a valuable scrapbook; R. A. Couey, former Superintendent of the California Street Cable Railroad Company, for data concerning James W. Harris; Jack M. Dodson, for valuable assistance rendered in connection with checking the manuscript; John William A. Hall, the oldest conductor, and George Mitchell, the oldest gripman, of the California Street Cable Line, for many anecdotes; Gelett Burgess for the use of his "The Ballad of the Hyde Street Grip"; Miss Jean Price, of the Library School of the University of California, for her research work in my behalf at the Bancroft Library; Miss Mabel Gillis, State Librarian at Sacramento, for furnishing me with many references; Lindley Bynum, for material from the Henry E. Huntington Library at San Marino; Phillip McLean, for information gathered in the Hopkins Transportation Library at Stanford University; Pardee Lowe, who collaborated with me on the chapter on Chinatown; the Society of California Pioneers for the use of several illustrations; and the California Historical Society for material on Andrew S. Hallidie.

I am indebted to friends who supplied me with a fund of personal information: H. M. A. Miller, C. O. G. Miller, John Freuler, Berthold Guggenhime, the late H. R. Williar, the late Albert Bender, Fred Pickering, the late Dr. Emmet Rixford, James K. Moffitt, Francis Farquhar, Edward O'Day, Richard Schmidt, Joel Hecht, George Berton, the late Miss Anna Beaver, John Cuddy, Leonard V. Newton, Walter Swanson, Louis S. Slevin, Fred G. Will, William Magee, Earl G. Ryan, George W. Gerhard, Mrs. Mary Taylor Beardslee, Charles M. Bufford, Michael Harrington, John Henry Mentz, and Fabius T. Finch.

I desire to express my gratitude to a host of other friends, too numerous to mention, for their helpful suggestions and criticisms.

Other historical information comes from sources listed in the bibliography.

E. M. K.

SAN FRANCISCO, CALIFORNIA
September 1, 1944

CONTENTS

LIST OF ILLUSTRATIONS

Cable Car Days in San Francisco

CABLE CAR DAYS

In San Francisco

CHAPTER I

SAN FRANCISCO OF THE 'SEVENTIES

SAN FRANCISCO of the 'seventies was a fog-shrouded, wind- and dust-swept city pervaded by a gaiety which only a contemporary of those days could have enjoyed. With the gold fever in its joints, the city suffered from growing pains. The precious metals taken from the hills still poured into its banks. The town had first clustered around its waterfront, but gradually the churches, residences, and business and manufacturing establishments had spread to the hills and the sand dunes to the west and south. Still the visitor was astonished by the grandeur of the Bay. Lagoons that had harbored windjammers and whaling schooners had been converted into plank streets. In the march of progress came steam-driven vessels from the Orient, Europe, and the East Coast. Already the swift clipper was fighting a losing battle.

For many years there had been a regular ferry service to the East Bay and daily trips up the Sacramento River to the capital. The smaller dwellings on Rincon Hill were surpassed by the

3

palatial Nob Hill residences. Nevertheless the eyes of the Argonauts were not completely blinded by the glitter of gold and their minds not entirely occupied by the exciting commercial pursuits. Dramatic art was flourishing, and the Grand Opera House and the California Theatre presented the best talent available from the East and from Europe.

San Francisco was the City of the West, the cosmopolis of a new world, abounding in happiness, prosperity, and opportunity. Along its streets walked the politician, his vest pockets bulging with nickel cigars; the democratic banker, his eye alert for business; and the prospector fresh from the hills. Money came from discriminating investors in London, Amsterdam, and Paris to take part in the growth of this precocious youngster.

With a population of less than two hundred thousand, already San Francisco's fame had reached to the far corners of the world. Had not the pioneer just reason to be proud and to rejoice in the progress the city made during the short interval since the state of California had become a member of the Union?

To house the newcomers, hotels were built that became as famous as the city itself. The Baldwin at Powell and Market, erected by E. J. ("Lucky") Baldwin, had a glamorous history spanning the years from 1876 to 1898. It was the gathering place of the city's elite and was a model of comfort and a rival of the Palace Hotel conceived and built by William C. Ralston.

The Occidental Hotel was another first-class hostelry that maintained an enviable reputation long after newer and finer hotels had become popular. Major William B. Hooper, its genial proprietor, was tireless in his efforts on behalf of his patrons. As a routine matter, he had vases of flowers and platters of fruit placed in their rooms as soon as guests arrived. These attentions found much favor, and many of his innovations were copied by his competitors. Hooper hired only waiters capable of taking verbal orders from a table full of guests and of carrying in their heads a hundred and one items without making a mistake.

What Cheer House was popular with the miners, farmers, and cattlemen who appreciated cleanliness, good food, and attractive prices, although this four-story brick hotel on the corner of Sacramento and Leidesdorff was not up to the standard of the gilded palaces just mentioned. Its founder, R. B. Woodward, was a smart Yankee who knew how to cater to his customers. He prospered and was able to acquire and develop the famous "Gardens" of delectable memory. This open-air recreation park covered two blocks of well-cared-for shrubbery, an artificial lake, fountains, and trees. Its particular attraction was "The Zoo," a perpetual delight to adults and children alike.

The great mining sections, such as the Comstock and Mother Lode, had been pouring out their treasure for years; millionaires blossomed forth overnight and faded from the scene almost as quickly, and the financial community was in a whirl of excitement. The effects of such unparalleled riches were widespread. These made San Francisco a financial center, and influenced the social life and molded the character of the city. Fifteen years of abnormal excitement, with gains and losses incredible in extent, at times had a tendency to unsettle trade and orderly business. Speculation became a habit.

The city for the most part was made up of three classes of residents: those who had made and still held their stakes; those who had made a fortune and lost it and were fighting to regain a place in the sun; and those who had never struck it rich but had fixed their dreams on the legends about those who had. In these three groups were the Spaniard, the Indian—the real native Californian—the American, the European, and the Oriental who had come in since 'forty-nine. If, without previous knowledge of his whereabouts, a person had been dropped in San Francisco's Portsmouth Plaza, he might well have been more bewildered than if similarly placed in any other part of the world.

This cosmopolitan aspect gave to San Francisco a charm and

an individuality. There were few places where money could be earned so easily or would purchase so much. The very heterogeneity of its people led to informality. Transactions mounting to thousands of dollars were closed by a clasp of hands over a drink. Only in such a city could an "Emperor Norton" live and carry on his delusions with pompous proclamations and demands for money for the treasury that existed only in his twisted mind.

Montgomery Street during the daytime was crowded with vehicles of many descriptions. The region of the retail shops extended from the foot of Telegraph Hill to Market Street. Gay, fashionably dressed women did their shopping at luxurious stores. There was the ever present "cabby" at the street corners. Along this street plodded the tinsmith calling "Tintimen," perhaps carrying in his money belt a thousand shares of penny mining stock that next day might be worth a thousand dollars. Rickety grindstones on wheels wobbled over the cobbles, their owners shouting, "Oho, get your razors ground." There was also the song of the orange vender: "Oranges, sweet Los Angeles oranges, two bits a dozen." Following the closing of the exchanges, the curbs about Leidesdorff and Montgomery streets would each day be crowded with cabbies, tinsmiths, venders, bootblacks, domestics, and ladies of uncertain reputation, all trading in stocks. On the Barbary Coast the gambler bet twenty-five on the queen, or the miner in from the creeks an ounce on the king, or the cattleman ten head of steers on the ace.

At night Kearny Street was brilliant and gay, the colorful dresses of the women making sharp contrast to the conservative broadcloth suits and beaver hats of the men. The cafés, theaters, and gambling halls were crowded. The daytime energy and the intense business activity accelerated in pace, if that was possible, for the night life. Saloons and bartenders were then taxed to serve their thirsty customers. The free-lunch counters were stacked with food to be had for the asking, representing a variety of edibles seldom seen on a family home table. In these bar-rooms would congregate editors, lawyers, doctors, judges—the community's most respected personages. No doubt there was an atmosphere of good-fellowship to be met with along the cocktail route of early San Francisco.

In August 1875 a mining-stock panic occurred, and share values declined approximately sixty millions of dollars. Several financial concerns, including the Bank of California, which heretofore had been regarded as impregnable, were forced to suspend operations. So great was the liquidation of securities that several exchange firms were compelled, temporarily, to close their doors. San Francisco's capitalists—men of the caliber of Fair, Sharon, Baldwin, and Keene—became unduly cautious and conservative in their appraisal of almost every enterprise, although their propensity to aid in the search for precious metals still remained. There was a disinclination to enter real-estate ventures, construct buildings, or make investments in unfamiliar enterprises. For a long time a lack of confidence and an un-willingness to back proficiency and inventiveness persisted.

The 1875 panic had swept away the life savings of many, the huge fortunes of others. There ensued one of the blackest pe-riods in the history of California. Into this scene came a dreamer. But this man did not dream of gold empire, nor had he the dreams of an "Emperor Norton." Andrew S. Hallidie had con-ceived the idea of operating a street railway without visible motive power—passenger cars drawn by an underground cable, to conquer the hills in a route to a new subdivision called the Western Addition; mechanical cars to take the place of the an-cient horse-drawn cars. Unheard of! The fantasy of a crank! Even in the East and in Europe there was no such thing. Un-heeding, grimly determined, Andrew Hallidie perfected the mechanical details that made his dream a reality. So and in such a setting the groundwork was laid for the first cable-car system in America.

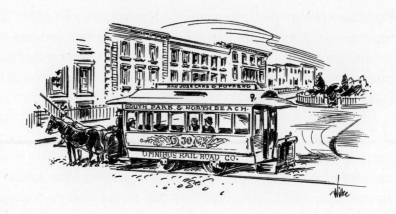

Chapter II

THE HORSECAR PERIOD

IN THE DAYS before organized transportation, horse-drawn buckboards, victorias, and carriages of various descriptions had been the principal vehicles used in San Francisco to carry people to their destinations.

The first attempts to make travel easier were made in 1850, when an eight-year franchise was granted for the construction of a plank-paved toll road on Folsom and Mission streets. The road originally crossed the Mission Bay Swamps at Seventh and Mission streets on a pontoon bridge, continued southward to Sixteenth Street, and terminated at Mission Dolores, thus linking the Mission settlement with the new town in Yerba Buena Cove. The construction of this first road had been expensive, and tolls ranging from twenty-five cents for a horse and rider to one dollar for a four-horse team were charged. The tollhouse stood at Post and Kearny streets and was later moved to a point near Fourth and Mission streets.

New developments soon took place. As early as 1852 the

first public conveyance, an omnibus service operated as the "Yellow Line" by Crim and Bowman, ran on a thirty-minute headway between the Post Office (Clay and Kearny streets) and Mission Dolores, by way of Kearny, Third, and Mission streets. The fare was fifty cents on weekdays and one dollar on Sundays. In 1854 another route operated between Third and Townsend streets and Meiggs Wharf (built by and named after colorful Harry Meiggs, whose all-too-bold business ventures brought him into conflict with the law, from which he escaped by a precipitate flight to Peru). In 1855 a third omnibus route covered the section between the Post Office and the Presidio. By 1857 other lines entered the field, chief among them being the "People's" or "Red Line," which ran in competition with the yellow-colored cars. At the same time fares were reduced to ten cents.

The San Francisco Market Street Railroad Company was incorporated in 1857 and was operated as the first street-railway system in the rapidly growing community, running from Battery Street along Market, out Valencia to Seventeenth Street. Originally the management had intended to run horsecars, but on account of the shifting sand dunes the franchise was amended to permit steam dummies. The railway commenced service on July 4, 1860. The company had a varied financial experience, was forced into receivership, sold under foreclosure, and eventually placed under the ownership of the San Francisco San Jose Railroad Company, then operating as a steam railroad between San Francisco and San Jose, with its San Francisco terminus at Valencia and Market streets. Awkward-looking "dummy" locomotives with one or two cars attached were operated by it on Market as far as Fremont. The town's main thoroughfare at that date was not graded, and the railroad passed through many narrow cuts in the sand hills and past ponds of stagnant water. On special occasions trains of the San Francisco San Jose Railroad continued along Market Street as far as the present site of the Palace Hotel, the locomotive preceded by a man on horseback ringing a bell or waving a flag and shouting, "Look out for the train!"

After 1867 steam-propelled cars were discontinued, and a horsecar service was inaugurated, running from the waterfront to Twenty-fifth Street. The new horsecars were spacious and well built—attesting the skill of local mechanics, for with the exception of the rails all materials used were produced and fabricated in California. As to their usefulness *Langley's City Directory* for 1867 commented:

It is hardly too much to say that the modern horse car is among the most indispensable conditions of modern metropolitan growth. It is to a city what steam car and steamship lines are to the state and country. In these days of fashionable effeminacy and flabby feebleness, one never walks when one can possibly ride. The horse car virtually frees the ultimate limits of suburban growth.

The coming of the horsecars to San Francisco was not hailed with much general enthusiasm, however. Contrary to the quoted opinion expressed by the publishers of *Langley's City Directory*, the pioneers were good, sturdy walkers and the distances were short. Even Sam Brannan, a man of vision, the owner of large sections of downtown real estate, was reported to have said: "Horse cars are not needed; they won't pay."

Frank McCoppin, for a long time identified with the management of the Market Street Railroad Company, in a letter written in 1894 records some of the conditions with which the company had to cope in the early years of its existence. It reads:

San Rafael, Calif.
July 11, 1894

Mr. Willcutt,

Dear Sir:

. . . . The franchise to build the Market Street Railway was, as you are aware, granted in 1857 to Thomas Hayes and his associates. Under the old constitution of California all such franchises were granted by the Legislature. The work of grading the roadbed was commenced in 1859 and the road was opened to travel in 1860. Where the New City Hall now stands [McAllister and Leavenworth] was then Yerba Buena Cemetery, which was approached over Mission Street [then a toll road] and 7th [then Price Street], which is in front of the new Post Office site. The lot never formed any part of the so-called "bog" of which so much has been said. The projector of the Market Street Railway owned what was then known as "Hayes Valley," bounded by Van Ness Avenue, Market, Haight, Pierce and Turk Streets, and the road was pushed in order to develop the land and bring it into the market. The old banking house of Pioche, Bayerque & Co. having a mortgage upon "Hayes Valley," deeming it to their interest to help the road, loaned the Company $100,000, and, as the road did not pay, it was ultimately sold for the debt and passed into the hands of the then owners of the San Jose Railroad, Messrs. Donahue, Newhall and Mayne, who subsequently sold both roads to the Southern Pacific. Indeed, I think it was not considered of large value at that time by the Southern Pacific people, and it was so to speak "thrown in" with the San Jose Road. I owned one-tenth, or 100 of the 1,000 shares; the balance was owned by Hayes, who subsequently turned it over to Pioche, Bayerque & Co. at fifty cents on the dollar—that amount being credited on his land mortgage. My interest was sacrificed under the foreclosure proceedings.

Along the entire line of Market Street from Hayes Valley to Third Street was a succession of sand hills in 1859. One of the largest was in front of the now famous Blyth Block [westerly gore of Market and Geary]. After they were cut through and the railroad started, we had much trouble in keeping the sand off the track. The cutting, for economy's sake, was narrow, and, as the sand dried in the embankments, it slid down and covered the tracks. This difficulty was finally overcome by the use of "brush" or scrub oak, which was utilized as a sort of thatch that covered and held the sand. At first the road terminated at 16th, then Center Street, but later, when Pioche & Bayerque got possession of the "Willows"—a then famous suburban garden—it was extended to a little beyond 17th Street to the entrance of the "Willows."

About the same time, the Hayes Pavilion at Hayes Park on Laguna Street was erected and a branch line along Hayes Street to Laguna Street was constructed. On week days this branch was operated by a one-horse car, but on Sundays and holidays the steam dummies with their cars ran up to the pavilion. . . . .

At the time the road was built, Hayes Valley was rented to Italian gardeners who raised there large quantities of vegetables. The block on which the St. Ignatius Church and College now stands [now Van Ness and Hayes] was the residence of Thomas Hayes, the founder of the road. Upon the adjoining block resided Mr. James Van Ness [author of the Van Ness ordinance], which gave title to all lands outside of Larkin and Ninth Streets to the Charter Line of 1851, Divisadero and 21st and Napa Streets.

I will here recite one instance of the enormous growth of the value of the property in this city. In 1861 I held in trust the title to the block upon which Mechanics' Pavilion stands now, bounded by Larkin, Hayes, Fulton and Polk Streets, and the owner sold it to Archbishop Allemany for $6000. Its present owners offered two-thirds of this to the Government for a Post Office site for one million dollars.

During the first seven years of its existence I was virtually the Market Street Railway Company, as one of its Directors, its Secretary, Superintendent, and General Manager. I was, in fact, what the law designates a "corporation sole"—the only corporation I ever knew that had one; but now, when I ride upon its cars like the rest of its patrons, I pay my nickel to the young gentleman [Colonel Charles F. Crocker] who in 1859-1860 was engaged in the picturesque employment of making mud pies in Sacramento. It is needless to say that during the period referred to the road was managed with ability, and if it did not prove profitable to its owners it was because there were but four or five dwellings in Hayes Valley and between that and the city proper only a single habitation, owned and occupied by Mr. Paul Rousett, a very worthy French gentleman, who subsequently died in his native country. The lot is now owned by Mr. Walter Dean. If the ghosts of the Pioneers who slept in "Yerba Buena" patronized the road, the treasury was none the richer on that account.

The apparent success of the little road excited the cupidity and envy of many persons who besieged all subsequent legislatures for franchises for street railways in every direction. In San Francisco all engaged to carry passengers for five cents. But the Legislature of 1864 was induced to increase the fares to six and one-quarter cents in tokens of four, costing 25 cents (single fare ten cents), at which figure it stood until 1876, when a member of the Senate from San Francisco introduced and passed an act reducing it to five cents.

In my time there were never any great strikes upon the road, nor was the passage of the U.S. mails ever obstructed or delayed. . . . . .

The Horsecar Period

The road had some picturesque and memorable features. Its road-bed along the center of Market Street from California to Third Street, being below grade, was called "McCoppin's Canal," in which, during the rainy season, many worthy citizens narrowly escaped drowning.

The only opening along Market Street west of Third Street was upon the line of the Railroad, and the daring owners of some vehicles had the temerity to drive over the Company's tracks; but that nonsense was put to a stop by digging several deep trenches across and under the tracks. Against this proceeding some unusually enterprising citizen filed a mild protest with the Board of Supervisors, which was promptly referred to the member for the Eleventh—the superintendent of the road—who as promptly reported against it.

Such was Market Street in those days. The property fronting upon it was of such inconsiderable value that its owners put up with the Market Street Railway and all its concomitants, including wheezy engines, canals, and trenches to obstruct travel.

FRANK MCCOPPIN.

In 1861 the Omnibus Railroad Company was reorganized by Peter Donahue, Michael Skelly, and associates as a successor to the "Yellow Line." The line ran from Sansome and Jackson to Stockton and connected with the North Beach. The road also connected North Beach with South Park, then San Francisco's aristocratic residential section.

Peter Donahue is responsible for this characteristic story: The Omnibus Railroad Company had a robust employee whose job it was to walk the tracks and inspect the rail connections. During the rainy season he would patrol Washington Street from Kearny to Stockton to keep the tracks sanded. The chap did his work exceptionally well, and Donahue, observing his conscientiousness, offered him a position at higher pay in the carbarn. His surprising reply was: "Just leave me alone, Mr. Donahue. I'm doing all right here, and this job just suits me." This loyal worker held on for many years and when he died he left a substantial bank account, some choice parcels of real estate, and a block of stock in the Omnibus Railroad Company.

This new road was soon nicknamed "Skelly's Line," after

Michael Skelly, its energetic, omnipresent superintendent, who was always on the job. He might be found at the Fourth Street barn, directing men, horses, and cars; later, at the northern end of the line, bawling out some delinquent driver; and, after the lapse of an incredibly short time, in the midst of a Folsom Street gang, helping with his brawny arms to tear up pieces of track—showing the boys how to make a good job of it.

Another story was told by Michael Skelly about an employee named Dan Curran, a colorful figure, known to everyone. Dan was stationed at Jackson and Kearny streets with an extra horse; it was his job to hitch this horse to the regular two to assist them in hauling each car up the hill to Stockton Street. Curran became so expert he could swing his horse into line and hitch it without causing a stop. At the top of the hill he would turn Dobbin loose to find his way to the foot of the hill and then would soliloquize as he followed:

D'ye know it's a grand thing that animil has human intilligence, or there'd be murther in this alley. D'ye know he hates a Chinyman worse than whiskey; but here he is in the heart of Chinytown and with Chinymen all around him and he niver tries to pommel 'em or bust up their stands, just because he knows he's on duty. But I tell ye, if he warn't on duty and there warn't no car to be pullin', that critter'd tear around here among them heythen and I shudder to think what he'd do to thim. Don't I know the time I had him on Third Street whin the Chiny laundry man poked him in the nose with a basket of washin'? Didn't I pay tin dollars for the washin' and five to the Chinyman?

The year 1861 saw the incorporation of the Central Railroad Company, with R. J. Van Dewater as president. Its capital stock was $500,000. The line developed into a quiet, prosperous concern which operated its dark red cars on schedule, never in a hurry, from Sixth and Brannan to Davis and Vallejo. One of the branches went along Turk to Fillmore Street, then out Post to Cemetery Avenue, now Presidio Avenue.

The growth of the city had been well marked by the construction of street railroads. The first lines traversed the most populous portions and as the advantages of each were developed and its profitableness was proved it was extended as rapidly as the population spread. The North Beach and Mission Railroad was built in 1863 under the guidance of Dr. A. J. Bowle, Robert Turner, and Michael Reese as a rival to the Omnibus Line. This paralleled some routes and consisted of three lines. One extended from North Beach via a zigzag route to Market Street, along Fourth Street to the Central Pacific Railroad depot at Townsend Street. These were yellow-colored cars. The blue line ran from the Oakland Ferries up California to Kearny, over to Market, and out Market to Eighth, over Eighth to Folsom, and out Folsom to Twenty-sixth Street. The third route, operating a red car, ran from Montgomery and California along Battery and First to Folsom and out Folsom to Eighth, and transferred to the blue line. The cars ran at five-minute intervals, and the fare was five cents.

It is not recorded whether or not all the early horsecars ran on schedule; but the following episode relates to horsecar railroading in San Francisco:

In the omnibus days there was a wonderful and fearful network of tracks, in the old downtown district. One day at noon an extra driver relieved the regular man at the carhouse of the Central Railroad Company. When the regular man returned from lunch his relief had not appeared. The relief man wandered around with his bobtailed horsecar taking every switch he came to, up Sixth Street to Market Street, along Taylor to Post, to Kearny, to Bush, to Sansome, to Jackson Street. Somewhere along the route he got on to the tracks of the old North Beach and Mission Railroad, went to the ferry, and on the way back got tangled up with the horsecar rails of the Omnibus Railroad Company on Washington–Stockton–Union Streets, and took in the North Beach District. They did not find that extra man and his bobtailed car until late that afternoon, and he was in an exhausted and bewildered condition.

In 1863 Isaac Powell, E. T. Pease, and R. B. Woodward saw a money-making opportunity in the operation of another horsecar line and incorporated the City Railroad Company. The line introduced the first light, one-horse vehicle, seating fourteen persons, serviced by a driver only and dispensing with the conductor. There were two branch lines using these new "bobtail" cars. The Mission Street Road ran along Mission to New Montgomery and Market, stopping at the then recently completed Grand Hotel. A string of blue "bobtail" cars called "Woodward's" operated from the Oakland Ferries up Market to Sutter, along Sutter to Grant, over Grant to Market, along Market to Fifth, Fifth to Mission, and Mission to Twenty-sixth Street.

Frequently when the cars were crowded passengers were compelled to cling to the stanchions with one foot on the step and the other dangling in mid-air. When the driver asked for their fares, many were unable to reach the coin box without passing the coins along the line of riders, all of whom enjoyed the proceeding. The rear door was controlled by a lever operated from the front platform, so that the driver could close it before starting, thus preventing the patrons from falling out of the car while it was in motion. The front platform was entirely enclosed by a semicircular dashboard, but passengers desiring to smoke were permitted to occupy it. The horses wore small bells that made pedestrians and other traffic aware of the approaching cars.

It was demonstrated by the City Railroad that this arrangement, with average receipts of fourteen dollars a day, paid better than the larger two-horse vehicles, since the company could cover the ground more frequently and with fewer employees. The innovation found favor with the public and soon superseded the larger cars drawn by two horses.

Another horsecar company was organized in 1866 called the Potrero and Bay View Railroad. This line used the Market Street rails from the ferry landing via Fifth and Bluxome to Fourth and Townsend, which was the terminus of one division of the line. At this point, a transfer was given to the cars of the other section, which ran on Kentucky and Railroad Avenue, crossing Mission Bay, the Potrero, Islais Creek, Butchertown, and continuing to South San Francisco. For a five-cent fare it was possible to travel from the foot of Market Street to South San Francisco, a distance of five miles.

The construction of this road was costly. It required the building of bridges across Mission Cove and Islais Creek, each of which was about a mile long. A deep excavation had to be made through the Potrero Hill, necessitating the removal of over one hundred thousand cubic yards of rock. The route was the most direct one to the Bay View Race Course on Hunters Point, and served an extensive and rapidly growing district. In 1876 the line became part of the Market Street Railroad system.

In 1870 R. B. Woodward and Henry Casebolt made a deal permitting the horsecars of the Sutter Street Railroad Company to continue from Ninth and Mission on the tracks of the City Line to the "Gardens," and in return the blue "bobtail" cars were allowed to run on Sutter Street from Grant Avenue to Sansome. This arrangement made Woodward's Amusement Park more accessible, and it became the favorite play spot of young and old. Woodward, carried away by the success of the company, offered his patrons a newly devised car described in the *San Francisco News Letter* of June 1870 as follows:

Mr. R. B. Woodward is deserving of great praise for his enterprise in giving us a novelty in the form of a new car. . . . . The Kimball Manufacturing Company has just finished for him the first "Street Palace" ever built here. This car is elegant in design, luxuriously fitted up with velvet carpet, and sofas extending the length of the car, upholstered in embroidered tapestry costing sixteen dollars per yard. The fresco painting work was done by a San Francisco artist, at a cost of two hundred dollars. The object of the car is to supply a want long-felt by the ladies, desiring to visit Woodward Gardens at hours when gentlemen are engaged and cannot accompany them. It being strictly a ladies car, no gentlemen will be admitted unless with ladies. There will be no disgusting pipe or cigar smoking on the platform, nor the usual

Woodward's Gardens in the early 'eighties

Market Street Railway Company, Valencia Street line;
corner Market, Post, and Montgomery streets

standing crowds to be squeezed, but every passenger will be seated. The fare will be ten cents, and it is worth the extra five cents to enjoy so much luxury.

Horsecar facilities were available from North Beach to the Mission, and as far west as Lone Mountain. From this point the journey could be continued to the Cliff House by Concord busses. In the 1864–1870 period the Cliff House was a world-famous resort and was spoken of both as an institution and as a landmark. Historically speaking, the Cliff House marked the end of the pioneers' journey across the continent and the terminus of the white man's westward march.

Various edifices covering approximately the same ground followed each other in succeeding periods, but to Sam Brannan goes the credit for having built the first. Its recorded opening was in 1858. The Cliff House of the early 'sixties was a little flat-roofed building, perched on the edge of the cliff. From the balcony, high above the breakers, one could gaze through a telescope at the seals or could sight ships beyond the Farallones. After several changes the ownership went to Adolph Sutro, who in the early 'eighties bought the property and most of the adjoining land. In 1894 the building was partly destroyed by a freak accident caused by an explosion from a vessel that met disaster on the jutting rocks below. In 1909 a new Cliff House was opened—a permanent building of concrete and steel constructed to withstand any contemplated catastrophe. At length there followed a period when its doors were closed for thirteen years; this time Prohibition was the cause. More or less renovated, it was reopened in 1937.

The Seal Rocks and Point Lobos (derived from the Spanish *lobos marionos,* meaning sea wolves) always have shared the fame of the Cliff House. Tourists from far and wide visit this landmark to obtain their first impression of the Pacific. They never forget the memorable view, the sunsets, and the ever present invigorating breezes, the latter in sharp contrast to the op-

19

pressive heat prevailing in many of the Eastern states during the summer months. The majestic clipper ships, as they entered the Golden Gate, furnished from this scenic point an enthralling spectacle to the tourists as well as to the local residents.

Another one of the early horsecar lines which was destined to become important was the Sutter Street Road, of which the City Front, Mission and Ocean Railroad was the forerunner. It was incorporated in 1863, and Henry Casebolt supervised the construction of the line. The first cobble was torn up at Sutter and Sansome in 1865, and by November 1866 six green cars were operating. A series of franchises granted over a period of twenty years extended operations on Sutter Street from Presidio Avenue to the Ferry and from Fourteenth and Mission (Woodward Gardens) to Market, to Larkin, and over Polk to a terminus at Broadway. A branch ran from Broadway and Polk via Vallejo, Octavia, Union, Pierce, Greenwich, and Baker to Harbor View, and on Pacific from Polk to Fillmore.

Henry Casebolt was endowed with both an inventive genius and an ambition to stimulate the operation of the company. He came to San Francisco in 1851 from Virginia and had acquired a reputation of being a man of great resourcefulness, desiring to hold a worthy place in the community, a leader in thought and in action. With a boldness based upon innate confidence, he constructed the main line, a double track, six cars, stables, and a car house for $72,500. His experience as a carriage builder proved valuable, and as an inventor he introduced many innovations, including a lever grip for cable car operations. On the first day receipts were only fifty dollars, and it was with no little discouragement that secretary David Wilder informed Casebolt that something drastic had to be done to stimulate traffic or the working capital would be depleted in short order. The company paid Casebolt in cash as long as there was money in the treasury; but he had to accept a mortgage on the property and $12,000 in stock for the balance due on the contract.

The Horsecar Period

It required no considerable business sense for Casebolt to realize that if he were going to get his investment out of the enterprise he must put up money, control the company, manage the property, and sacrifice all other business interests. Casebolt borrowed most of the $10,000 needed to buy the right-of-way from the City Front, Mission and Ocean Railroad in order to tap the ferry travel. The Central Railroad tried to block this move, claiming that the Sutter Street concern had no rights on the city front covered by the Central's franchise. A battle royal in court followed, which ended with the Sutter Street Railroad Company's victory.

During the first year's operation Casebolt had advanced to the company over $42,000, which the directors attempted to repay in greenbacks worth only sixty cents on the dollar. Casebolt was compelled to purchase stock in the open market sufficient to give him control and obtain recognition of his just claim to payment in gold. In 1871 he obtained a franchise extension and greatly improved operating conditions by giving special attention to the requirements of lady patrons, who heretofore had been put to considerable inconvenience by uncleanliness and highly uncomfortable seating arrangements.

In 1871 Casebolt built the "balloon car," characterized by its oval outline and its novel construction, which enabled its upper body to turn freely upon the supporting stationary truck. It was a horse-drawn vehicle with a two-row seating capacity of six or seven passengers each. When the car reached the end of the line, the motive power would take a hearty drink from a conveniently placed trough, the driver would remove a pin and direct the horses in a semicircle, and, presto, all was ready for the return trip. This novelty was an excellent substitute for a turntable and saved the driver a lot of trouble hitching and unhitching. About 1874 the "balloon cars" could be seen on Larkin Street, Ninth to Mission, and Mission to Fourteenth streets, where was the entrance to Woodward Gardens.

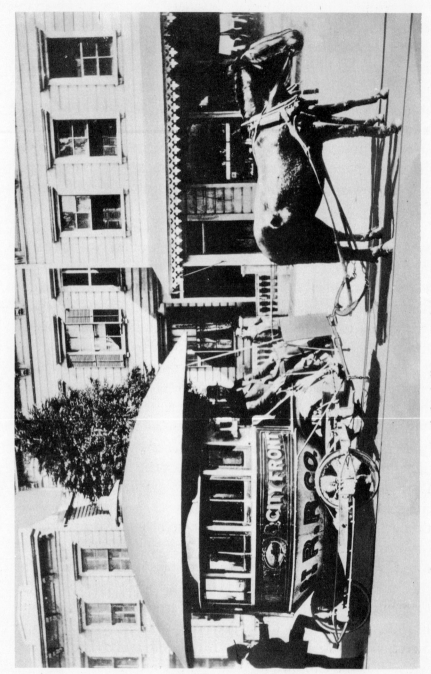

Casebolt's balloon car of the 'seventies

The Horsecar Period

In 1875 the controlling interest in the Sutter Street Railroad was purchased by Robert Morrow and Maurice Schmidt for $37.50 a share. The road under Casebolt's management had increased its receipts until it was earning $1,100 a day and had become the most profitable in the city except for the Valencia Street Line of the Market Street system. During 1877 the Polk and Larkin Line was operated in part by cable and the remainder by horses. At Larkin and Sutter, the open dummy was uncoupled from the closed car and horses were hitched to the latter for the rest of the trip. It was in January 1877 that the Sutter Street Wire Cable Railroad was formally opened. Ten years later, in 1887, a strike interrupted service. The platform men were working twelve or more hours a day for $2.25. A demand for a pay increase to $2.50 and a reduction in working hours to a maximum of twelve was refused—apparently not because the road was unprofitable but because the company was determined to keep the men on existing low wages and long hours. Public sympathy was with the strikers, especially when it became known that some of the persons in the company were using the strike and the loss of earnings resulting from the strike as an excuse for depressing the stock of the company.

Robert Morrow was primarily interested in stimulating traffic in order that his substantial investment might become a lucrative one. The following story illustrates the problems which gave the early-day cable-car operators no end of trouble.

Morrow hired detectives Hogan and Rogers to keep an eye on a conductor named McCarthy. It was apparent to Morrow that his young conductor was leading a rather fast life. McCarthy was frequently seen riding out to the Cliff or the Park behind a double team, always in company with some gaily dressed woman but seldom twice with the same one, going to first-class restaurants, ordering expensive dinners, drinking high-priced wines, and having a good time generally—all on a salary of two dollars and a quarter a day. Gossip had it that he was

23

the son of a millionaire who had just fallen heir to a fortune and that he was spending his easily acquired money freely. Morrow knew differently; he was aware that the conductor under suspicion had no legitimate source of revenue other than his pay check.

After three months of following McCarthy, detectives Hogan and Rogers arrested him on charges that he was robbing the company by not turning in all the cash collected on his run and that he sold transfers which he had stolen from the superintendent's office, entrance to which he gained by use of a skeleton key in his possession. Needless to say, McCarthy was promptly discharged after a short life but a merry one with the Sutter Street Wire Cable Railroad.

Generally speaking, the attitude of the people was favorable to the horsecar companies. Nevertheless, it was commonly thought that the superintendent of one of the early horsecar lines was in the pay of blacksmiths and buggymakers, because the rails of horsecar lines were laid hurriedly and at such an elevation above the street's surface that carriages were dislocated or their wheels were broken off by contact with the rails. At any rate, the demands of an irate citizenry were so great that the Board of Supervisors at one of their regular meetings in September 1875 appointed a committee to investigate and ascertain the validity of the complaint.

In 1875 the way was being prepared for the evolution to the cable-car systems and the death knell of the horsecar had rung. Gradually the lumbering, easygoing old horsecars, with their smoky, dingy oil lamps which threw a sickly glare over the rows of passengers, and their jingling bells and picturesque drivers began to disappear.

By 1875 the horsecars had reached the crest of their popularity. Their service had been good and was appreciated by the riding public. Generally, single fares were ten cents and six and one-quarter cents in cards of four, and the old method of collection continued: Tickets were printed on strips of pasteboard and each ticket as used was clipped off with a pair of scissors.

Frank McCoppin, recognizing the need for a uniform fare in San Francisco, introduced in 1877 a bill in the state legislature fixing a five-cent rate for all lines. The belief was generally held that a uniform five-cent fare would help the development of the city. There was little opposition on the part of the transportation companies to the passing of the act.

The Board of Supervisors had given out franchises with a lavish hand and on the easiest terms to almost anyone who asked for one. Consequently several franchises had been granted, apparently not for the purpose of building a road but to be sold at some future time to the highest bidder.

Enough has been written to show the background against which the coming of the cable cars occurred. The history of the horsecar period was one of continual friction, competition, and growth. By 1873 there were eight horsecar systems operating.* There were eighty miles of single track, and transportation facilities were increasing rapidly with the opening of additional streets and the development of new districts.

All lines seemed to have a common feature—sociableness prevailed. There was a genial relationship between the employees and the traveling public. Everything moved at a slow tempo. Schedules were not scrupulously followed. The horses jogged along at a leisurely gait, hearing but not heeding the driver's occasional "Cl'k, cl'k." There were no platform signs admonishing "Do not talk to the driver." The carmen knew nearly everyone who rode. Patrons swapped jokes, gave tips on mining stocks, and complained of the prevailing corruption among the local politicians. In the rear the conductor was watching for passengers. If a housewife signaled that her husband would be out as soon as he had drained his coffee cup, the driver

* See Appendix, Table 1.

occasionally would wait. It was not unusual on the last run to the stables for a dozing or inebriated passenger to instruct the carman to deposit him right at his doorstep, for there was no rule forbidding a stop in the middle of a block to take on or let off passengers.

As the city grew, "hay burners" gradually became less satisfactory as motive power. Frequently the animals proved unequal to the load, and occasionally, owing to accidents, the passengers had to get out and push the car back on the track. Inevitably horsecars began to disappear and cable cars, San Francisco's innovation and invention, its own institution and pride, took their places. Now for the first time a way was found to overcome San Francisco's steep hills and residents who made their homes on Nob and Telegraph hills no longer had to wade through the sand.

CHAPTER III

ANDREW S. HALLIDIE

THE START OF THE CLAY STREET
HILL RAILROAD COMPANY

A CHAPTER in this story belongs to Andrew Smith Hallidie, the mechanical genius who originated cable-railway transportation and devoted nearly half a century of his life to San Francisco's progress. He was born in London on March 16, 1836. His paternal grandfather, a Scotch schoolmaster and a soldier during the Napoleonic wars, had served at Waterloo. His father, Andrew Smith, had been born in Scotland in 1798; and his mother, born Julia Johnstone, also was from Scotland. Andrew Smith was an engineer and inventor. His patents for the making of wire ropes, granted from 1835 to 1849, were his most important achievements. Young Andrew Smith later adopted the surname Hallidie in honor of his godfather and uncle, Sir Andrew Hallidie, who had been physician to King William IV and to Queen Victoria.

His early training was of a scientific and mechanical char-

27

acter and at thirteen years of age he was working in a machine shop and drawing office operated by his brother, thereby gaining the practical experience that stood him in good service the remainder of his life. In the evenings he continued his studies, but manual labor during the day and study at night began to undermine his health. He was full of life, fearless, fond of adventure, and gifted with an inquiring mind and a good memory. His father, who had some interest in the Frémont Estate in Mariposa County, decided to take him to California.

In 1852 father and son arrived at Clark's Point in San Francisco. The younger man promptly became a mining prospector and for the next three or four years tried his hand at mining, first with pick, pan, and rocker, then with long tom and sluice. With his mining activities he interspersed other work, such as blacksmithing, surveying water ditches, roads, and trails, and building bridges. At the age of nineteen he constructed a wire-suspension viaduct over two hundred feet long across the middle fork of the American River.

In 1856, utilizing one of his father's inventions, he began the manufacture of metal rope, and by 1870 A. S. Hallidie & Company had commenced the fabrication of wire cables in an unpretentious building at Mason and Chestnut streets.

In 1867 Hallidie took out his first patent covering the invention of a rigid suspension bridge, and in the years that followed he took out numerous patents for other inventions. Among them was the "Hallidie Ropeway or Tramway" for transporting ore and other material in mountainous districts by means of an elevated endless traveling line, which he had invented in 1867. Hallidie informs us: "from 1868 to 1870 I was experimenting on a system for the transport of material over mountainous and difficult regions by means of an elevated traveling wire rope, effectively demonstrating in various places previous to 1873 that the Hallidie rope-way was practical and successful."

Andrew S. Hallidie

He experimented with wire ropes for drawing heavy loads. He foresaw that one of the greatest drawbacks to the successful operation of the system he contemplated would be the breaking or mutilation of the cable during its hours of use. He developed a crucible steel cable with six strands of nineteen wires each, each individual wire .062 inch diameter, with a tensile strength of 160,000 pounds per square inch, and capable of bending over its own part with a round turn, straightening out, and repeating at the same spot without fracture.

In a comparatively short time A. S. Hallidie & Company built up a splendid reputation for efficient workmanship and quality products. By 1878 there were three cable-railroad companies in operation, all of which bought their cable from Hallidie's company. Since the guaranteed life of a wire cable was only twenty months, the outlook for the manufacture of cables was excellent.

In 1871 he completed plans by which streetcars could be propelled by underground cables, the idea having come to him during an accident which had occurred in the winter of 1869. One evening during a walk he had paused to watch an overloaded streetcar start up one of the steep hills. A cold rain had been falling all day, and impatient men and women had crowded the little car until there did not seem enough room for the proverbial "one more." Slowly, and with the utmost difficulty, the four horses had moved the car. When half a block had been covered, one horse had slipped on the smooth cobbles. The driver had instantly applied his brake, but with such force as to snap the chain. The car at once began to slide backward down the hill, dragging the bodies of the unfortunate horses over the stones, until the vehicle had reached the level of a cross street, where it was stopped. As Hallidie assisted in releasing the mutilated animals he determined to work out a means of making such accidents impossible.

At that time Hallidie had already successfully installed a

number of ropeways in the mining districts of California. His devices permitted great iron buckets containing rock and ore to be carried across deep chasms and up steep mountain sides where it was impossible to build bridges or roads. He undertook to adapt the same system to the propulsion of streetcars up the hills of his city. The enterprise called for an endless wire rope, under ground, to which a car could be attached and from which it could be released at will. In one year Hallidie worked out the problem. The next step was to secure the necessary capital for a demonstration. People laughed at the scheme, and no one could be found who would invest in the undertaking. Yet discouragement served only to make Hallidie more determined, and at his own expense he had a survey made for a line up California Street between Kearny and Powell, a distance of 1,386 feet.

In his notes he wrote:

About the time I had matured my Ropeway system, my attention was called to the great difficulty experienced in hauling the street cars (or tram cars) up one of the steep streets of the City of San Francisco, and the great cruelty and hardship to the horses engaged in that work. With the view of obviating these difficulties, and for the purpose of reducing the expense of operating street railways (tram-roads), I devoted all my available time to the careful consideration of the subject, and so far matured my plans that I had California Street (a very steep street in San Francisco) surveyed in 1870 by an engineer of the name of David R. Smith, and in the *Sacramento Record,* a newspaper published in the City of Sacramento, California, in 1870, a statement is there published in its telegraphic news of what I proposed to do, viz: to run a rope railway to carry passengers from the city to the plateau above.

It was intended to be an experimental line. Unfortunately, D. R. Smith was called to Central America on some railroad work and the plan was temporarily abandoned.

During the subsequent twelve months Hallidie succeeded in interesting only three men—these from among his friends and business associates—to go along with him in his project. Even they were dubious about the feasibility of the project and were induced to participate under the pressure of a strong friendship. Their names were Joseph Britton, of the well-known firm of lithographers and map makers, Britton & Rey; Henry L. Davis, a former sheriff of the City and County of San Francisco; and James Moffitt, of the long-established wholesale paper house of Blake, Moffitt & Towne—all of whom had been associated together in the building of the Mechanics' Institute. With their assistance a company was organized in 1872, and Clay Street, instead of California Street, was selected, as offering lower construction costs and a generally more suitable location. Accordingly, a franchise was obtained, a new survey was made, and subscriptions for the purchase of stock were invited.

The public responded to the extent of only one hundred and twenty shares. Even those few shares were soon turned back to the company, so great was the force of unfavorable public opinion, concurred in by the very best engineering talent in the West.

Periodical spells of discouragement seized the three men. Hallidie would spend hours using convincing arguments to show that the plan would actually work. A circular was issued carefully describing the undertaking. An office was opened in the Clay Street Bank Building and a working model placed on exhibition there. Finally, by persistent solicitation through canvassers among the property owners on the hill, pledges totaling $40,000 were obtained, to be paid in upon completion of the project. However, pledgors to the total of only $28,000 met their obligations. Hallidie himself contributed $20,000, all he had, and his three friends about $40,000. An additional $30,000 was secured by a ten-year loan bearing 10 per cent interest through Mr. Burr, of the Clay Street Bank, and a mortgage on the property was given as security.

Meanwhile the expiration date of the franchise was approaching, and the cable road still existed only in the fertile mind of its inventor—and there everybody assured everybody else it

Clay Street Hill Railroad Company in the 'seventies

would ever remain. Yet in May 1872 money matters were finally arranged, and courageously, although with precious little encouragement, Hallidie started his engineering task. Each day brought a new difficulty to solve. Undreamed-of problems swarmed out of the so-called "hole in the ground," until a less-determined man would have given up in despair. Patterns had to be devised for the machinery and the numberless parts—all by the one man on whom rested the responsibility for ultimate success or failure. Some years later Hallidie modestly wrote:

I cannot recount here to-day the many obstacles that had to be surmounted, but they all have been overcome. At that time, they seemed very great indeed, and I do not doubt, if I had been less familiar with the problem than I was, and had less confidence than I did, it might have been many years before the cable system would have reached the point of practical application.

At length the first day of August 1873 was approaching. If on that date no cable car was running, all rights would expire and everything would be lost. It was part of the plan to take a passenger car from any of the streets of San Francisco, convey it to the top of the hill by the grip car, and transfer it to a connecting horse line; this, however, was impracticable.

Desperate efforts to complete the building of the cable road were made, and at a little past the midnight hour on July 31 a few tired, nervous men met at the powerhouse located at the corner of Leavenworth and Clay streets. All night, with feverish anxiety, they had been watching the final, hurried efforts of the workmen.

Within the powerhouse, furnace fires roared under the boilers, which were blowing off their overload of hissing steam. At last all was ready. The engine started, very slowly at first, and as the tension took up the slack of the several thousand feet of cable, the steady hum of the endless rope was heard in its long tube under the surface of the street. At five o'clock in the morning on August 1, 1873, the group, consisting of Hallidie, his three partners, his draftsman, William Eppelsheimer, Assistant Superintendent P. H. Campbell, and the bookkeeper, Thomas P. Burns, stood at the top of the Clay Street hill at the crossing over Jones Street. The grip car had been dragged to its place here. On it the brakes—crude, straight levers pressing on the wheels—were applied and found to be effective. The grip, Hallidie's invention—operated by means of a screw and nut on a hand-wheel—fastened its jaws securely on the cable. The final moment of success or failure had arrived.

Day was breaking. A dense fog was coming through the Golden Gate and rolling over Nob and Russian hills. The bottom of the steep Clay Street grade was obscured by this early morning mist. From the open slot near the middle of the street came a mysterious rattle. Hallidie listened intently, nodded with an air of satisfaction, and ordered "All aboard!"

The workmen next pushed the car forward to the brow of the hill at Jones Street, where the slot and tube commenced. One of the most careful and intelligent employees was selected to handle the levers. "Jimmie," shouted Hallidie, "are you ready?" Jimmie peered down into the fog bank and, thinking of the steep descent of several hundred feet, turned pale. His courage failed him; he shook his head, and backed off the car.

The others now began to show signs of uneasiness. Then Hallidie, assuring them there was no cause for alarm and quickly springing to the levers, picked up the cable, and the car and its human freight descended slowly into the mist below.

The bottom was reached in safety, the grip having been tried several times on the way down. The car was stopped at the crossings, then started again; the cable was repeatedly dropped and picked up; and various tests were made. At the bottom of the hill at Kearny Street the so-called "dummy" was reversed by means of a turntable, the grip was again fastened to the cable, and off went the car up the Clay Street grade again.

The successful test was accepted soberly. It was a solemn

affair, and only a round of silent but hearty handshakes gave expression to the men's feelings. The town was asleep. An enthusiastic Frenchman thrust his night-capped head out of a window as the car went by and threw toward it a faded bouquet; his was the only demonstration. It was then decided to make an official trip in the afternoon.

The morning experiment had shown the necessity of carrying the car as far as the engine house. Therefore the cable line had to be extended one block further west. This additional construction work could not be done without obtaining the necessary permission. For this reason further operation was to be stopped as soon as the official trip had been made.

That afternoon many of the prominent city officials and businessmen came up from Montgomery Street and assembled at Clay and Kearny to witness the first public trip. Mayor William Alvord and Chief of Police Patrick Crowley lent dignity to the affair. Fire Chief David Scannell, Sheriff James Adams, and Supervisors Timothy McCarthy and Samuel Taylor in turn acclaimed the invention and congratulated Hallidie. The police were helpless in curbing the crowd. Too many friendly hands pushed the car on to the turntable—the impact broke a bolt connecting the grip with the car frame. The mishap caused a delay of twenty minutes. Some expressions of regret were heard, intimating "the thing had proved a failure." As soon as the repairs had been made, the people rushed into the car and on the dummy, some hanging on to the guardstrip, others actually climbing to the roof.

The car was a crude affair as compared with the present coaches designed in 1906; but it was the father of them all. The 1873 tram was rather small and appeared somewhat top-heavy, since it was built to operate on a narrow-gauge track. The dummy, built to seat ten to twelve persons, together with the car itself, intended to accommodate fourteen or more, carried ninety passengers on the first run.

The first cable train, September 1873

Eastern terminus of the Clay Street Hill Railroad Company

Everything went well until the steep grade above Powell Street was encountered, when the car stopped. Hallidie soon found the cause of the trouble. The grip pulley, that had been freshly covered with tar, a too effective lubricant, was slipping over the cable. Lime and sawdust that happened to be at hand were thrown on the cable, however, and the car and its load were safely hauled to the top of the hill.

At the foot of the incline there was a double turntable. The space was so limited that considerable ingenuity had to be exercised to insure its operation. When the dummy car reached the bottom of the hill, it was uncoupled and run on the turntable, the slot allowing the shank of the grip to pass freely. A few minutes were consumed making these shifts; then away went the dummy and the passenger car up the steep grade, finishing the first round trip in short order. Thus a milestone in the progress of street transportation was established, to the lasting credit of Andrew S. Hallidie and his associates—Joseph Britton, Henry L. Davis, and James Moffitt.

After a great deal of research and experimental work, the Clay Street Hill Railroad was able to make further progress in the safety, efficiency, and economy of its operations, the effect of which was undeniably beneficial to traffic as well as to the development of adjoining property. The city authorities and residents were well satisfied as to these points. The pioneer stage had been passed, and the road was an acknowledged success.

When this first cable railway became commercially successful and brought fame to Hallidie, William Eppelsheimer pressed a claim for a share in the achievement. The resulting patent litigation created considerable ill will, as Eppelsheimer had acquired his familiarity with the cable patents while working as a draftsman for the Clay Street Hill Railroad Company. Armed with affidavits from Henry L. Davis and Joseph Britton—both men of the highest standing—Hallidie proved that Eppelsheimer's pretensions to a claim were absolutely unfounded and that all the fame and merit properly belonged to Hallidie, who had taken out his first grip-pulley patent in 1870 and had followed it in short order with a great number of related inventions.

Hallidie lived to see the fruition of his many years of strenuous efforts. Many of his inventions were used, and the collection of large royalties for a lengthy period made him wealthy. In later years he enjoyed relating how he lost a substantial sum through an oversight. In spite of being thoroughly familiar with the problems involved, and after years of experimenting with the cable system, he had overlooked the importance of patenting a slot sufficiently narrow to keep out carriage wheels. Only the prompt but expensive shift to a narrower slot had made it possible to operate cable cars on city streets.

Hallidie deservedly took his place among San Francisco's honored citizens and devoted much of his time to the general welfare of the community. He gained recognition and prominence through his participation on the platform and in the press in the discussion of the burning issues of the day. His brilliant articles on labor organization and kindred subjects attracted wide attention. His energies also were directed toward promoting educational progress. He served as chairman of the Finance Committee of the University of California and associated himself with the Mechanics' Institute. Much of the credit goes to Hallidie for laying the solid foundation upon which this latter organization was established. He was deeply interested in manual training and was one of the leading spirits of the California School of Mechanical Arts and of the Wilmerding Training School. In 1878 he was elected a member of the Board of Freeholders to frame and propose a charter for the City and County of San Francisco, and was re-elected to this in 1886.

The name of Hallidie is perpetuated in the Hallidie Building, on the north side of Sutter Street between Montgomery and Kearny streets. Within the entrance of this building is a plaque bearing the following inscription:

Clay Street Hill Railroad Company, car and dummy showing wheel grip

Andrew S. Hallidie

HALLIDIE BUILDING
NAMED IN HONOR OF
ANDREW SMITH HALLIDIE
BORN IN LONDON ENGLAND
MARCH SIXTEEN 1836
DIED IN SAN FRANCISCO
APRIL TWENTY-FOUR 1900—
CREATOR OF OUR CABLE RAILWAY—TWICE
MEMBER OF A BOARD OF FREEHOLDERS
CHOSEN TO FRAME A CHARTER
FOR THIS CITY—REGENT OF THE
UNIVERSITY FROM THE FIRST MEETING
OF THE BOARD JUNE NINE 1868 TO
THE DAY OF HIS DEATH—DURING HIS
LAST TWENTY-SIX YEARS DEVOTED
CHAIRMAN OF ITS FINANCE COMMITTEE
BUILDER   CITIZEN   REGENT
A MAN OF INTEGRITY

The unprecedented success of the Clay Street Hill Railroad created a rush for street-railway franchises. The news leaked out that the monthly net earnings on Hallidie's line were averaging $3,000, amounting to 5 per cent per month on an expenditure of $60,000. The earnings were derived from five-cent fares, and the business was growing. It was such information which prompted the speculators on Leidesdorff Street, the realtors on Montgomery Street, and the mining brokers on California Street to ask the Board of Supervisors for franchises, which were granted almost without question, without the requirement of any payment and without any agreement to pay a certain percentage of gross earnings into the city treasury. Many syndicates were formed to gobble up franchises which cost them nothing but promised great future returns.

In November 1877 a group acting for undisclosed interests secured a franchise to build a line on Geary Street. This new company was called the Geary Street Park and Ocean R.R. Co., and the Central Railroad was behind it. Service commenced on February 1, 1878, from Market and Geary, then westward to Presidio Avenue. A steam dummy continued on Point Lobos Avenue (now Geary) over First Avenue to Golden Gate Park. The cost of converting the road from horse to cable power was $275,000. The money necessary for the project was raised in the usual manner—a substantial amount by stock subscriptions and the remainder by monthly assessments.

Passing mention should be made of the Presidio and Ferries Railroad, which was organized in October 1878. Among the principal stockholders were Alex. Baldwin, Antoine Borel, Joseph Britton, John and Edward Coleman, Sidney Cushing, A. E. Kent, James Moffitt, Albert Miller, and Robert Watt. This line was the direct route to the northwest part of the city. A horsecar (part of the system) ran from the Ferry up Jackson to Montgomery Street and returned by way of Washington Street. Cable cars were used along Montgomery Avenue, and Union to Steiner. Another portion of the line, from Steiner to Baker, terminating at Harbor View, near the present site of the Palace of Fine Arts, was operated by a steam dummy. The cost of constructing the cable section was $190,000. In later years, with the expiration of the franchise, this cable line became part of the Municipal Railroad of San Francisco.

Under the old traction system, one horse, on nearly level tracks, might draw approximately forty passengers; but the work of the cable car in conquering the inclines could not have been performed by a hundred horses. Many families that had been keeping horse-drawn vehicles discarded them, preferring the quicker and less bothersome travel by cable car. It was not many years before hilltops which had been waste areas covered with drifting sands became the sites of fashionable hotels and expensive apartments, thus causing real-estate booms of tremendous proportions and rapidly bringing new wealth to thousands.

CHAPTER IV

LELAND STANFORD

THE BEGINNING OF THE CALIFORNIA STREET CABLE RAILROAD COMPANY

LELAND STANFORD, in 1874, conceived the idea of adding another cable line to San Francisco's rapidly growing transportation facilities. He discussed his ideas with Mark Hopkins, Lloyd Tevis, David Colton, and Charles Crocker. All enthusiastically agreed that his plan would definitely furnish Nob Hill dwellers with a desirable transit convenience, but not all agreed that it would prove to be a desirable investment.

Stanford instructed E. J. Robinson, the son of Robert Robinson, head of the Law Department of the Central Pacific Railroad Company, to draft a franchise—not an easy matter in view of the difficult requirements that had to be met. There was to be no interference with the ordinary wagon and carriage traffic; the street surfacing was to be left undisturbed; there was a stipulation that the vehicles used be under constant control, so that they could

43

California Street Cable Railroad, 1882

be started or stopped at any point on the route as quickly as a horsecar; the speed was set at not less than three miles and not more than eight miles an hour; and the fare must be five cents per passenger for the entire trip.

Robinson managed his task with consummate skill. Such a franchise, approved by Mayor A. J. Bryant, was issued on June 14, 1876, granting to Leland Stanford, Mark Hopkins, David Porter, Edward Pond, Michael Reese, Louis Sloss, David Colton, Charles Crocker, Isaac Wormser, D. O. Mills, and others the right to operate the California Street Cable Railroad Company. Seldom had a similar undertaking been sponsored by an equally imposing group of men of wealth and prestige.

Stanford, determined to get as many influential men as possible interested in his venture, solicited stock subscriptions from that group. The stockholders' roster included most of his incorporators. Charles Crocker refused financial participation, but allowed his name to be used as one of the grantees of the franchise. D. O. Mills, who had come to California from New York in the flush time of gold nuggets, faro, and navy revolvers, was too involved in the intricate problems of the Bank of California to dissipate his energies on five-cent fares. His refusal to serve as a director was a disappointment to Stanford. Mills was needed because he moved among men of the finest type in American leadership, commanding the respect and confidence of all. John H. Redington and Michael Reese took the same position as Mills. Mark Hopkins expressed the opinion that the investment was too large to be returned in five-cent pieces, and was quoted as saying: "It is just as likely to pay a dividend as the 'Hotel de Hopkins'," referring to his residence then under construction. Stanford subscribed for the stock that his associates did not want. He was greatly disappointed that his friends in the Market Street Railroad, then a horsecar line, did not play along with him, as he had hoped that the experience accruing would be of mutual benefit to both groups. There is no exact information available as to the amount of stock Stanford had to take, but good authority has it that he owned approximately four thousand of the five thousand shares. While Stanford's private thought might have been to operate the system as a hobby, the enterprise proved profitable from the outset.

Isaac Wormser, who owned about two hundred shares, became the first treasurer but, owing to some differences with Stanford, soon resigned and was succeeded by Captain N. T. Smith. An interesting story is related about Wormser's retirement. It is said that from the very inception of the cable line the management received numerous complaints from residents in the neighborhood of the carbarn, then located on Larkin Street, that their Monday "wash" was blackened by smoke and soot belching from the smokestack. They requested that the chimney be raised an additional thirty-five feet. Wormser believed the request a reasonable one and advised compliance, but Stanford disagreed. Thereupon Wormser decided that he would rather not be identified with a company that had so little regard for the public. Later, when Stanford perceived increasing antagonism to his otherwise unopposed venture, he yielded to the request of the "neighbors" and abolished the smoke nuisance at a comparatively small cost to the company.

In 1877 Stanford met Henry Root, a Vermonter who had come to the Coast in 1864 and whose abilities as an engineer were well known. In Henry Root's *Personal History and Reminiscences* is found the following paragraph:

On the day appointed I was asked to go along to take a view of the intended route. Most of the incorporators were there, but Crocker and Hopkins were conspicuous by their absence. Later in the day Isaac Wormser invited the whole party to his house, where a champagne celebration took place. The site for a new powerhouse was talked over, and it was left to P. H. Canavan and myself to select one and to report our decision to Stanford. At this time it was apparently taken for granted that I was to be the construction engineer.

Geary Street, Park and Ocean Railroad Company steam train
during the 'eighties

California Street Cable Railroad Company, corner California
and Powell streets, 1880

A preliminary estimate set the cost of the enterprise at $350,000, which amount included a concrete roadbed from Kearny to Fillmore Street, an engine house, a carbarn at the southeast corner of Larkin and California streets, and the necessary rolling stock. The company was capitalized at $500,000, with five thousand shares of $100 par value. The construction costs amounted to $430,000.

Root's most important task was to surround himself with a competent staff, and accordingly he proceeded to hire the best talent obtainable. He engaged as draftsman George Watriss, who had done commendable work on engine and steamboat designing. The choice for superintendent and assistant superintendent fell upon Stanford's friends Thomas Seale and A. H. Wands, respectively. T. J. Thomas was selected as head carpenter and model maker, and soon became Root's right-hand man. William H. Milliken, foreman in the Central Pacific's Sacramento shops, was appointed master mechanic. George Hare, who was shop foreman, after some disagreement left the company in 1881, but returned later and in 1904 became secretary, serving until 1934, when he was elected vice-president, which position he held until his death in 1935. The company was also fortunate in securing for the grip-and-brake division the services of George W. Douglas, the best-qualified man in the country for this department.

Ground was broken on July 5, 1877. Men started work on the road construction just east of Larkin Street. The work progressed rapidly, and the last rivet was driven on November 12, 1877.

Certain engineering difficulties had to be overcome. The street grade was uneven, and there was the problem of keeping the cable a uniform distance below the grip. Also, there was the problem of keeping the heavy rains out of the tube and the dirt from clogging the slot. The slot had to be sufficiently wide to permit the passing of the grip lever and yet narrow enough to prevent ingress of solid objects which might interfere with the movement of the cable or with the operation of the pulley. A new rail had to be designed by Root. He submitted the design to the Cambria Steel Company in Pennsylvania for a cost estimate, but this concern refused to entertain the order, it being too small to justify installation of the new rollers that would be required. Root reported his difficulty to Collis P. Huntington, who reassured him, saying: "They will roll them for me. Let me have the blueprints, the specifications and the diagram of the cross-section and I will attend to the order when I get to New York." This promise was kept, the order was placed in April 1877, and the rails were shipped overland from Johnstown. They were made from a good quality of light-weight steel after a new pattern, their cross-cut resembling a T. The invoice price ran to about $20,000, which was the only part of the construction funds spent outside of California.

Root carried out Stanford's wish to build a first-class road surpassing any other streetcar line then existing. The construction of the roadbed was unique. Metal forms had to be molded and placed in concrete by an entirely new method. Delays were encountered, not only in perfecting the machinery but also in building the cars and breaking in the gripmen.

Hallidie, who controlled a number of patents covering every phase of cable-railroad construction, indicated to Stanford that if the Clay Street crowd received a proper compensation (understood to have been about $30,000), they would join him and his associates in building the California Street Line. Moreover, the Clay Street group was willing to subscribe for one-half of the capital stock, provided the construction plans met with their approval. To this proposal Stanford briskly replied: "If I undertake to build the California Street road I am going to be the one to determine what plans will be used and if our lawyers say that we are infringing on patents we will pay, if we must, for the privilege of using them."

Eastern terminus of the California Street Cable Railroad in the 'eighties

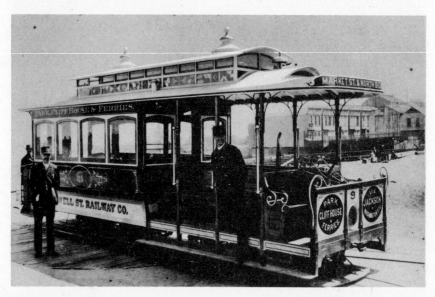

Powell Street Railway Company, North Beach line

Looking up Powell Street from Sutter, about 1890

Shopping-bound on the Sutter Street Wire Cable Railroad in 1877

The Clay Street directorate thereafter remained aloof and Stanford told Root that he would not pay a cent until he had to. Hallidie's patent rights turned out to be sufficiently inclusive to compel payment of $30,000 by the California Street Cable Railroad Company for a license to operate under them. The legal annals of that period are replete with records of other lawsuits of one cable company against another for patent infringements and the failure to pay license fees. None was carried to a successful conclusion.

The powerhouse engines were built by Wallace W. Hanscom, of the Hope Iron Works in the Potrero, from drawings made by George Watriss. They were of the upright type, 750 horsepower, and constructed so as to propel the cables at a maximum speed of eight miles an hour. The machinery was housed at the corner of Larkin and California streets, the main shaft extending out into the middle of the street so that the main driving gears could be placed in the center of the railroad track. The original boilers were of the locomotive type and were constructed by Hinckley, Spiers and Hayes. William H. Birch & Company, then located at 110 Beale Street, furnished a considerable part of the machinery. Mechanically inclined individuals would gather at all times of the day to observe the power unit, so great was the curiosity and interest in the original way the drive shaft operated. At Kearny Street and at Fillmore Street underground excavations, sixty feet long and walled with solid masonry, contained automatic tightening gears designed to take up the slack caused by any permanent stretching of the cable which might occur.

Twenty-five cable cars and dummies were purchased. Approximately half of these were manufactured by the Kimball Manufacturing Company of San Francisco, and the rest were built in the Central Pacific shops at Sacramento. The cars, a newly improved, light-weight model, were quite attractive. The vehicles weighed only two thousand pounds, compared to the present-day weight of similar conveyances of eleven thousand pounds. At first a two-vehicle combination of car and dummy was used, with a seating capacity of twenty passengers. Later improvements increased the seating capacity to thirty-four. It is of interest to note that this cable-car company was one of the first subsequently to make use of the telephone, thus in no small measure facilitating its operations.

The opening of the California Street Line for public use took place on April 10, 1878. San Franciscans were fond of celebrations, in the manner of young and growing communities. The dedication was attended by over six thousand curious citizens, and was conducted in a style befitting the occasion. Many of the principal places of business were closed, and a large number of city officials turned out to pay tribute to Governor Stanford, the moving spirit of the enterprise. There were good reasons for this joyous manifestation. Property owners in the "Western Addition" were for the first time furnished excellent transportation, and the favorable influence of this upon real-estate values soon became obvious.

The California Street cable system was the crowning achievement of its class. The arrangement of the cars instantly met with the approval of the riding public, as no expense had been spared to make the road safe and perfect in every way.

The endless cable passed around large wheels at the termini of the line. The movement of the cable depended upon the speed of the powerhouse engine: since the heavy wire rope had a tendency to stretch, causing it to slip, a device known as a tension wheel operated to take up the slack. The cables ran over pulleys and through tubes cut in the city streets. The tubes were completely covered except for a narrow slot. A steel arm known as the grip reached through the slot. At the end of the grip was a metal band which clutched the moving cable. The grip was operated to tighten gradually so that the speed of the car could be accelerated by degrees. Throwing the lever forward released the cable to run free through the jaws of the grip. Henry Root invented the grip used on the California Street Line. Later James W. Harris perfected certain innovations which improved the operation of the grip.

Occasionally a gripman would "lose the rope," as the expression went and would be unable to retake the cable. When this happened the conductor and the gripman would politely request able-bodied passengers to "shove her across." Thus a patron might have to give up a bit of physical energy along with his five-cent fare.

Broken strands were the bugbear of the cable engineer. They caused not only much trouble and expense but danger as well. Incidental breakdowns were due to the jamming of the tension pulley caused by cracked strands of the wire rope. The piece of damaged cable had to be cut out and the ends spliced; therefore, inspectors continually watched the moving cable entering the powerhouse in order to detect any fault that might develop. When a broken wire strand interrupted the service, passengers usually were advised that it might be from thirty minutes to three hours before resumption of service could be expected.

Three kinds of brakes were used on the cable line. There was an iron brake which operated directly on the front wheel; a track brake, which was made of the softest kind of pine and wore out in a week or ten days; and an emergency brake, used when the other brakes were rendered useless. The force of this latter brake, jammed into the cable slot, was sufficient to raise the car from the track.

In contrast to the first-class construction work done on the California Street Line, Stanford instructed Superintendent Seale to finish the extension from Fillmore Street to Cemetery (Presidio) Avenue in a less pretentious manner. This decision was due to the light patronage expected from that section and also to the desire of the directors to build the additional unit out of earnings and not resort to a bond issue or stock assessments. They also wished to continue their liberal dividend policy. This economizing in the cost of building the branch road proved to be a mistake, and after a few years the extension had to be rebuilt and brought to the better standard.

An interesting side light on San Francisco's streetcar development in those years is contained in a letter which David Oliver, a lifelong resident of the city, wrote during that period and which is here reproduced almost in its entirety:

Broadway had been the leading street from the ferry. When the Central Pacific Ferry landing was changed in 1875 from Vallejo and Davis Streets to Market Street, the latter street became our main thoroughfare.

Beyond Webster Street everything was sand dunes. There were several blocks built up to the north as far as Washington. Nearly every resident in those days walked to work and to the theater. It was a common sight on Sunday to see large numbers of our respected citizens walking the three and one-half mile stretch of the old Point Lobos Road to the beach.

When the California Street Cable Railroad was built, my father rode to Kearny Street daily. I went to my place of employment on foot. We were thrifty in those days and we saved our nickels for Saturday night entertainment.

The California Street Cable Company employed as conductors and gripmen a fine, gentlemanly type. The visitors not only enjoyed the experience of a ride, but were impressed with the "folksiness" of the conductors, and their politeness shown in assisting old ladies on and off the cars. Their duties varied from acts of chivalry to ordinary toil. Their tasks ranged from calling streets to registering fares, making change quickly, and guessing the ages of the children.

I recall young Platt, a truly handsome fellow, son of Reverend W. H. Platt, of Old Grace Cathedral. There was quite a rivalry among the young ladies of well-known families living on the Hill for the privilege of riding the cars on which Platt carried on his duties. Rumor had it that the daughter of one of our wealthiest families had to be sent East in order to break up a budding romance with the cable car Adonis.

On February 14, 1879, the franchise was extended for fifty years. Permission was granted to operate steam dummies from Presidio Avenue and California Street to the Cliff House.

Cable Car Days in San Francisco

April 10, 1879, saw the California Street Cable Railroad Company celebrate its first anniversary. The citizens could not imagine why one car after the other was decorated. Some individuals vaguely suggested perhaps it was the birthday of Mayor Bryant. Later the community learned that the display of American flags was to commemorate the birthday of the finest wire-cable road constructed in America. Approximately eight thousand passengers a day were carried over its three miles of track. The success of the road had exceeded the most sanguine expectations of its projectors.

The rivalry between the managements of the California Street Cable Railroad and the Clay Street Hill Railroad grew with the increase in competition. Hallidie never quite forgot the insult which Stanford had flung at him when Hallidie had been refused the privilege of consulting with Stanford. On the other hand, the payment of $30,000 to Hallidie for the purchase of patent rights was ground for animosity on Stanford's part that never healed. In June 1879 the directors of the California Street Cable Railroad extended to the management of the Clay Street Road an invitation to have a free ride in order that they could see how a wire-cable road should be operated. The subtle offer went on to say that if it were accepted the Clay Street crowd would receive sufficient pointers to enable them to make a real cable line out of the Clay Street affair within a hundred years or so. The California Street Cable Railroad directors naturally were proud of their accomplishments. The road had the advantage of running along the street most notable for fine improvements. The cable cars made fast time, covering the distance from the eastern terminus at Kearny to Fillmore Street in nineteen minutes. The management spent money freely in the construction of the road and placed the streets in excellent condition through the use of redwood planks or macadam. From its inception, the California Street Cable Railroad became a popular one.

Chapter V

ANTOINE BOREL
THE CABLE CAR DURING THE 'EIGHTIES

IN 1884 Antoine Borel and his associates formed a syndicate to purchase the Stanford interest in the California Street Cable Railroad Company. Stanford was endowed with exceptional business acumen, and it was his habit in business ventures to bargain effectively. The stockholders in this venture received twenty dollars a share in excess of their original investment.

For the next thirty years Antoine Borel controlled the destiny of this important line. Born at Neuchatel, Switzerland, in December 1840, he was educated in the public schools of his native town and in higher institutions in Germany and Switzerland, where he specialized in the study of agriculture and industrial management. At the age of twenty-two he arrived in San Francisco and entered the private banking house of his brother, Alfred Borel, which had been established in 1852. His career turned out to be highly successful. His exceptional business ability made his advice greatly sought after in the financial af-

The Geary Street, Park and Ocean Railroad, 1900;
Geary Street east from Powell

United Railroad Company, Jackson Street line

fairs of many Western corporations. He served on the directorates of the California-Oregon Power Company, the Los Angeles Railroad Company, the Spring Valley Water Company, and the Bank of California. He never desired to hold the presidency of any of the corporations in which he served as a director. In 1898 Alfred Borel withdrew from active business and Antoine continued the firm under his brother's name. For nearly forty years Antoine Borel represented Switzerland as its consul. Because of this position and by reason of his leading place in financial matters, he was the acknowledged leader of the local Swiss colony.

Borel in 1884 persuaded his close friend, Charles W. Mayne, to take charge of the newly acquired traction concern. Mayne's unusual ability had been early recognized by Stanford, who had induced him to leave Belloc Fréres, a prominent private banking firm of that period, to join the executive staff of the Central Pacific Railroad Company. His experience there eminently fitted him to become manager of the Cable Company, and he served in this capacity from 1884 to 1888.

At the annual meeting of the Cable Company held in 1884 and participated in by directors Antoine Borel, Robert Watt, C. W. Randall, Jerome Lincoln, C. Denervaud, and Thomas W. Hinchman, the capital structure was increased under Borel's sponsorship to a million dollars, represented by ten thousand shares. An assessment was levied on the stock at the same time to raise the money for certain necessary improvements.

Borel frequently consulted his friend and financial adviser, Jacob Barth, a prominent stockbroker and member of the San Francisco Stock and Bond Exchange. An expansion policy having been decided on after careful deliberation, the brokerage firm of J. Barth & Company was entrusted with the task of placing $950,000 of 6 per cent first mortgage bonds—quite a sizable issue in those days—with the banks, insurance companies, and their clients. Bonds which were not disposed of by J. Barth &

Company were taken by A. Borel & Company for their clients, a large number of whom lived in Switzerland.

The money secured from the bond issue was used in the construction of the Hyde Street branch of the California Street Cable Railroad Company. The construction of this roadbed was started in 1889 under the direction of James W. Harris. The management boldly built a circuitous route from O'Farrell and Market along O'Farrell to Jones, to Pine, to Hyde, then northward to Beach Street. A short segment ran along Jones from O'Farrell to Market. Service commenced on February 9, 1891, and the line operated for several years without earning enough to pay platform wages. Gradually property values increased, transportation facilities stimulated building, and the popularity of the line was assured. New cars were ordered, with instructions that all materials used be bought from local firms.

In 1889, the car house was moved from the southeast corner of California and Larkin streets to the southwest corner of California and Hyde streets. J. C. H. Stut was the engineer in charge of setting up the machinery in the carbarn. Borel was the custodian of the cash and the securities of the Cable Company from 1884 to 1915, and upon his death in 1915 these duties were taken in charge by J. Henry Meyer & Company, the successors of A. Borel & Company.

When Charles Mayne resigned in 1888 on account of poor health, James Burgess Stetson was elected president. Stetson came of Colonial ancestry. At the age of twenty-one he journeyed around the Horn to join his father in California. He went directly to the Mother Lode and started gold mining near the town of Columbia. Luck was with him; he made $280 the first day. From mining he drifted into hardware merchandising, and eventually returned to San Francisco and rose to prominence. He served as president of the California Street Cable Railroad Company from 1888 to 1911, and during that time was instrumental in adding the Hyde Street branch. After the fire of 1906

Stetson gave up all outside interests and devoted his undivided attention to the Cable Company.

San Francisco's cable lines influenced the city's social life to a marked degree. Sunday, for instance, was always a gala day for the street railways. In the morning the various religious services on California Street were attended by churchgoers, who used the cable line in one direction and then enjoyed the exercise of a lengthy walk back to their homes. Also great crowds would gather in Golden Gate Park. Concord stages and surreys could be seen in large numbers on Old Point Lobos Road (Geary Street) headed toward the Cliff House. The trip meant a rather long, dusty outing in summer and in winter often turned out to be a very tedious ride through a bleak, fog-shrouded section.

People would also flock on Sundays to the cemeteries to view the magnificent mausoleums and the elaborate gravestones and well-kept plots. These cemeteries were popular as places to pass the day. Even courting was not considered out of place in these rather incongruous surroundings.

Groups of young people passed their Sundays at the beach and at Lands End. On special occasions exhibitions, such as balloon ascensions and parachute drops from a height of two thousand feet by "Professor" Baldwin, attracted thousands, who took the Cliff House cars to Bakers Beach to view this thrilling sight. For days afterward Baldwin's daring jump would be one of the chief topics of conversation. Another thriller for the crowds was the performance of Captain Jack Williams, who once spent a week on Seal Rocks. He was said to be the champion scientific swimmer of the world.

The streetcar managements of these days had an excellent eye for business. They employed acrobatic artists of the type of Millie Lavelle, who thrilled thousands of pleasure-seekers with spectacular acts. This entertainer, hanging by her teeth, would slide down a wire rope stretched from the Cliff House to the beach. The Davidson brothers, whom many San Franciscans

Geary Street Cable Railway

Telegraph Hill Cable Railroad Company, Greenwich Street, 1884

recall as two daring young tightrope walkers, gave awe-inspiring exhibitions on a rope reaching from the Cliff House to Seal Rocks. Many were their hair-raising feats performed high above the dashing breakers. The compensation paid these performers was never revealed, but there is good reason to believe that it was quite modest. However, the entertainment beyond a doubt served to increase the streetcar patronage to a marked degree.

Few residents of San Francisco have any knowledge of the unique cable-car line that operated to the summit of Telegraph Hill. Work on this enterprise was begun in February 1884, by the Telegraph Hill Cable Railroad Company, which later was often spoken of as "Layman's Folly." Frederick O. Layman, the promoter of the scheme, had succeeded in interesting Charles Kohler, Jacques J. Rey, and Adolph Sutro in the venture.

A single track with a short turnout was laid from Powell Street up Greenwich, intersecting Stockton, Dupont, and Kearny streets, overcoming a rise of one foot for each three and one-half feet—the steepest roadway in the world. An engine room occupying a space thirty-two feet square was hewed out of solid rock, and a boiler and two engines each of eighty horsepower were installed. The service was started on Sunday, June 30, 1884. Transfers were exchanged with the Omnibus Railroad Company, and a single fare took passengers from Mission Street to the top of Telegraph Hill. An observation car provided its riders with an unobstructed panorama. On the summit Gustav Walter and associates built a four-story resort with an observation tower affording sightseers a rare vista of the city and the Bay. The pavilion forming a part of this structure was used for serving refreshments, for dancing, and for other entertainment.

In spite of the many attractions supplied, Walter's pavilion, as well as the car line itself, operated continuously at a loss and in a few years both were abandoned.

In September 1887 an imposing group of directors consisting of W. J. Adams, John Ballard, Henry H. Lynch, Thomas Magee, and William H. Martin formed the Ferries & Cliff House Railroad. There existed the need of a cross-town road, and this influential and energetic group organized themselves for that purpose. At about the same time the Clay Street Hill Railway was purchased for $200,000 by the syndicate and was merged with the Powell and Jackson Cable Railroad. Thus for the first time property on North Beach was made accessible, and rents and values there improved. A new franchise gave the consolidated company the right to operate cars along Sacramento, Clay, Washington, and Jackson streets and also from the Baldwin Hotel at Powell and Market along Powell Street and then over Mason to the North Beach. Permission to operate a steam dummy from Presidio Avenue out California and around the cliffs to Point Lobos Avenue was likewise granted. This was a popular line not only on Sundays but also on moonlight nights, when the public would take it to the Cliff House, the Sutro Baths, and the Hotaling Pavilion. This cable road made available to the public picnic, fishing, and camping grounds and at the same time opened up the sand wilderness that extended from Presidio Avenue to Thirty-second Avenue, giving to all classes rapid transportation to the city's outer limits.

All San Francisco is familiar with the Market Street Railway's Fillmore Street Hill line running until recently on a very steep incline between Broadway and Marina Boulevard. Even though operated by methods representing improvements over those used prior to 1915, it had still to be regarded as antiquated and cumbersome. Abandonment and replacement by busses on Steiner Street had been frequently considered, and inevitably the line would have to be discontinued. By 1944 abandonment had been effected.

Although by 1886 cable transportation had been perfected to a marked degree, accidents were on the increase. The greater speed and the unusual steepness of the hills traversed were contributing factors. Frequently wet tracks, which caused car wheels and track brakes to slip, offered the major problem. This was finally overcome by the use of an auxiliary brake invented by an Australian, the new emergency device stopping a car within twenty feet. While minor accidents were fairly numerous for many years, very rarely did a serious one occur.

The pioneer Omnibus Railroad Company converted their horsecar operations to cable in December 1886. The line ran on Howard Street with a branch on Tenth, to Polk, to Grove, to City Hall Avenue, to Leavenworth, and to Post, and terminated at Montgomery and Market. The advantages of the cable car over the horsecar were quite obvious. The cable cars not only eliminated the cruelty to which animals were subjected in drawing heavy loads up steep grades in bad weather but permitted substantial reductions in operating expenses. In the late 'nineties the Omnibus Railroad was electrified.

Many a rider on the Powell Street Cable Line has wondered how a cable car goes over the top of the hill and how one cable line can cross another with such ease. The intersection of Powell and California streets presents all of the difficulties of such a crossing.

For taking a Powell Street car up the hill from Pine Street, the platform man grips and holds the cable tightly, and at the top of the hill, near the California Street track, he "lets go" by releasing the grip. Thereby he avoids raising his cable high enough to foul the California Street cable. At this point the car has acquired sufficient momentum to carry it beyond the full width of California Street, where, with the aid of the brakes, a stop is made to take on or let off passengers. Then the car drifts downgrade without requiring the cable, and at the next intersection the grip functions again and the car, re-attached to the cable, proceeds on its way.

The presence of snow on San Francisco's streets is so infrequent that when an occasional snowstorm does occur the novelty is thoroughly enjoyed by many of the city's population. The

Stock certificate used in 1884 by the California Street
Cable Railroad Company

Western terminus of the California Street Cable Railroad Company

morning of February 6, 1887, ushered in such an event. At the dawn of that day a great scenic transformation took place when Nature generously supplied the streets with a pure white carpet. Hilarious crowds assembled outdoors. On Nob Hill and in other residential sections of the city there was not a block which did not swarm with revelers. All dignity was laid aside. Well-directed snowballs of all sizes went whizzing through the air. The passing cable cars were made special targets, and so were the gripmen on the open dummies. There was no protection for them against the fusillade, and the best they could do was to button up their coats and "take it on the chin" or wherever the hits scored. The conductors also came in for their share, and many a snowball went crashing through the car windows to the dismay of the passengers.

James W. Harris was then superintendent of the California Street Cable Railroad Company. In spite of his efforts, he found it impossible to maintain the schedule. By noon the snow became slushy, and when it became too soft to pack some hoodlums threw slush mixed with gravel. As a consequence one of the gripmen nearly lost the sight of one of his eyes. Superintendent Morton, of the Market Street Cable Company, made the statement that most of the car windows on his line had been shattered. Yet nothing was done about it, and the bombardment of the cable cars, the breaking of windows, and the knocking off of high hats furnished thrills remembered for years by the fun-loving populace.

The California Street Cable Railroad Company was justly proud of its excellent crew of employees. Still not all of them were trustworthy. In the latter part of 1888 the management became aware of losses through the dishonesty of some of its conductors. "Spotters" were placed in advantageous positions along the road and in the cars, but every method to detect the fare beaters was unsuccessful. The matter was turned over to John Curtin, a most efficient detective. Curtin took several trips over the road, riding with employees who had been above suspicion. He discovered that a few conductors, when stopping in front of old men, women, or inattentive persons to collect fares, instead of "pressing the punch" as the rules of the road required would ring an appliance concealed in their sleeves. Eventually the detective made an arrest, and the accused conductor, when brought before his employer, confessed that he was the originator of this ingenious mechanism, called a "brother-in-law," and demonstrated how it worked. The device was being sold at seven dollars apiece to other pilfering employees. The exact amount of money stolen from the company by the aid of this device was naturally not ascertained; but all the dishonest employees were promptly dismissed.

There is no way to verify the following tale, but the yarn is worth repeating.

"Haven't got any change!" said the cable-car conductor.

"Neither have I," replied a gentleman after he had handed a five-dollar gold piece to a California Street cable-car conductor.

"Well, then, I will keep the 'fiver' until you get the change. I am here to collect fares, and not to make change for every bloated bondholder who pokes gold at me." And keep it he did.

The gentleman, having an important engagement, alighted on Powell Street and made note of the number of the car, expecting to be able to catch the conductor on his round trip from Presidio Avenue and get the $4.95 due him. After keeping his appointment, he posted himself at the corner of Powell and California to wait for the car to return. It did return in time, but with another conductor in charge, who informed the owner of the five-dollar piece that the man who had been on duty in the forenoon was only a relief man and there was no telling when he would show up again.

The victim, feeling that this was a new dodge and wishing to see the matter through, spent three hours more scrutinizing the ticket "punchers." Just as the clock struck six and he had given up all hope of seeing his man again, his patience was rewarded and his conductor appeared. He confronted him, saying:

"Here's my fare; give me back that five dollars you got from me this morning."

"What five?" asked the conductor.

"What five? Oh, you want to give me the forget act, do you? I have been waiting six hours for you and now if you don't come through I will spoil your face for you and have you thrown in jail into the bargain."

He got his change, but made a resolution always to have small change in his pocket for streetcar fares.

"The men on the line" were required to be polite and attentive to passengers, to answer proper inquiries, and to render assistance to ladies, children, and infirm persons in getting on and off the cars. This rule has given the employees of the California Street Cable Railroad Company a fine reputation.

Berthold Guggenhime, a prominent citizen, had the following comment to make concerning his experience:

It was more than fifty years ago when I started using the California Street Cable Company almost daily. Naturally, I became acquainted with the men on the line. There were no autos in those days to compete with the company. The people were quite charming and more hospitable than they are at present, but still it was not the practice then to give passengers who were waiting for the cable cars rides in passing carriages.

I got to know the gripmen and conductors. My wife was under a doctor's care and for lengthy periods she was an invalid. Occasionally she had to go down town. Together we would board a cable car and it was gratifying to observe how gently both the gripman and conductor assisted her on and off. Unquestionably the crew represented a high class run of men. Ever since then I cultivated the habit of sending packages of dried fruit or similar tokens of appreciation to the families of these old-timers in the Christmas season.

Rigid observance of regulations was demanded by the management, and infractions resulted in penalties. The runs were usually made on strict schedule. If a conductor in his haste to make up lost time failed to pay attention to a patron beckoning him to stop, the irritated would-be passenger would often give vent to his anger in no uncertain language. Some would carry their complaints in open letters to the newspapers, giving expression to their harsh criticism of the management. On the other hand, the rule forbidding conversations between patrons and the crew often was more honored in the breach than in the observance, and the exchanges of pleasantries were many.

The story is told of a method used by the Sutter Street Cable Line to check on the efficiency of conductors in collecting fares. A spy, in the person of a young and fashionably dressed woman, would board a cable car and when asked for her fare would politely reply in sweet tones that she had already paid it. To dispute this charming lady would have been a breach of gallantry, but if the conductor did not insist, next morning he would be severely reprimanded for neglect of duty.

An incident is recorded of a well-known lady living on Nob Hill who boarded a California Street cable car and produced five coppers in payment of her fare. Although pennies were quite uncommon at that period, they nevertheless were legal tender. The conductor at first refused to accept them, but when the lady insisted, he took them and tossed them out in the street, remarking: "Never mind, madam, I'll pay your fare." She indignantly reported the case to the management, and the next morning the conductor was given a two weeks' "vacation" without pay.

CHAPTER VI

NOB HILL HOMES IN THE 'EIGHTIES

ONE BY ONE the builders of the Central Pacific Railroad came from Sacramento and located in the city by the Pacific. Eventually Stanford, Hopkins, Huntington, Crocker, and other millionaires selected what is now Nob Hill on which to build their mansions and to pass the last years of their lives in the enjoyment of the fruits of their labors. Occasionally a writer would refer to the new district as "Snob" Hill. The public frequently spoke of the peak as "Knob" Hill; but after 1870 the "K" was rarely used. Many wealthy residents of South Park looked in the direction of Nob Hill when the "Second Street Cut" which divided Rincon Hill into two half cones was projected, and endangered the beauty of the then most aristocratic residential district. The introduction of the California Street Cable Railroad and a growing appreciation of an unsurpassed marine view prompted other prominent families to move to the crest of the California Street eminence.

As early as 1874 Leland Stanford had chosen the southwest

71

corner of California and Powell streets as the location for his magnificent residence. It was not surprising that Mark Hopkins, Stanford's closest friend and business associate, purchased the remainder of the California Street block extending in a westerly direction to Mason Street. There S. C. Bugbee & Sons, the architects engaged to draw the plans for the Stanford show place, were told to erect a palatial structure regardless of cost. They did so. The furnishings likewise were exquisite, including works of art gathered from famous European palaces.

Mark Hopkins, not to be outdone by Stanford, employed Wright and Saunders as his architects and built a residence the splendor of which had not been equaled on the Pacific Coast. It was distinguished by its unusual size and its characteristic gray towers, which could be seen from all parts of the Bay. The beautiful gardens were kept with the greatest care.

Mark Hopkins was born in 1813 in New York state and came to California in the days of the gold rush. San Francisco had had little appeal for him, and he had gone to Sacramento, where he had entered the grocery business. In 1855 he had formed a partnership with Collis P. Huntington. It was in the office of Mark Hopkins that the transcontinental railway plans were first discussed.

Mark Hopkins came to an untimely death in March 1878. His pretentious Nob Hill dwelling was never occupied by him. The house was closed for a number of years, when his widow went East and married an interior decorator named Edward Searles. Searles at length inherited the Hopkins home and eventually presented it to the San Francisco Art Association to be utilized for its school. Today the Hotel Mark Hopkins occupies the site.

Charles S. Crocker was another pioneer associated with the cable-car venture. He was actively connected with the construction of the Central Pacific, and for this reason did not desire to be an important factor in the management of the California

Nob Hill Homes in the 'Eighties

Street Cable Railroad Company. He was born September 16, 1822, in Troy, New York, where he received his early training in the public schools. His father's business reverses and resulting privations developed within him at an early age the habit of thrift, which trait he characteristically retained through life.

In 1875 Charles Crocker completed his home at California and Taylor streets, where he might enjoy a much-needed rest as well as the continued association of his friends, the members of his former Sacramento syndicate. The contrast between his show place on Nob Hill and his former home, a slate-roofed cabin ten by twelve feet on the bank of the Sacramento River, was frequently referred to by him in conversation with his intimates. Unfortunately the pressure under which Crocker had lived during the construction period of the Central Pacific seriously impaired his health and contributed to his early demise.

William Crocker, the son of Charles, built his California Street residence on the western end of the block between Jones and Taylor streets. The two Crocker mansions were destroyed by the fire of 1906, and the valuable block was presented to the Episcopal Diocese for the site of Grace Cathedral.

Old-time residents on the Hill recall an unusual meeting which took place in the vicinity of the Crocker mansions on the evening of October 29, 1877. The gathering, a protest affair, was led by the labor agitator, Denis Kearney. Several thousand men out for vengeance and voicing threats clashed with the serenity of the surroundings. These sand-lot gatherings of the Working Men's Party of California had been increasingly demonstrative. The agitators had become more radical and incendiary in their speeches.

Crocker, in his desire for an entire block of land for the site of his home, succeeded in buying all the adjoining holdings except a small lot owned by an undertaker named Yung. Crocker, regarding his undertaker neighbor as a nuisance, offered a substantial price for the property; but when Yung demanded an excessive figure, Crocker, rather than submit to extortion, raised a high wall, which almost completely surrounded Yung's house. This act prompted the meeting of Kearney and his gang, who attempted not only to tear down the "spite fence" but threatened Crocker with personal violence. As a result Kearney and some of his companions were placed under arrest for disturbing the peace.

With the death of General David D. Colton on October 10, 1878, another of the California Street Cable Railroad incorporators passed away. The Central Pacific lost its attorney, San Francisco one of its dearly beloved citizens, and Nob Hill one of its prominent residents. He took great pride in his mansion, known as "Colton House," one of the magnificent features of the California Street Hill. "Colton House" occupied the north side of the street, on the western half of the block, between Mason and Taylor streets, and was copied from a marble palace in Italy. It was a wooden structure painted white to suggest marble. The interior was filled with works of art from all parts of the world, selected with judgment and care. The library contained many rare books and was the delight of every scholar who entered it. "Colton House" was spoken of as one of beauty, luxury, and happiness. After Colton's death the property was purchased by Collis P. Huntington.

At that period Huntington stood out as another captain of industry with a conspicuous background. He had left New York because in 1849 that city had seemingly become overcrowded and he believed the West offered greater freedom of action. With enough money to carry him through a year of uncertainty and with a large amount of merchandise, he embarked for California. On account of disrupted sailing schedules he met with considerable delay at the Isthmus of Panama, and utilized the interval to carry on a lucrative business. Opportunities presented themselves to trade in equipment and supplies needed by the army of miners and prospectors of those days. Soon after arriving in Sacramento, he was enabled to lay the foundation of his great fortune, and his limitless ambition carried him to a height of industrial attainments approached by but few of his contemporaries. After Huntington's death the site of his mansion was eventually transformed into an attractive park.

On the northwest corner of Mason and California streets stood a bare, rough, rocky shoulder of earth whence a visitor could obtain a superb view of the city and its environs. He could look down upon structures of various sizes and shapes with jutting domes and spires and steeples. He could see busy wharves and a harbor crowded with ships of many nations. Berkeley, Oakland, and Alameda stood across the Bay, and beyond stretched the hills of the Coast Range to become lost in the hazy distance. It was in 1883 that James C. Flood selected this Nob Hill location for his residence. The site was leveled, Mason Street was cut through from California to Sacramento Street, and in two years his brown sandstone mansion was completed. The property was set off by a beautiful hand-wrought brass fence constructed by W. T. Garratt at a cost of $60,000. A caretaker was charged with the sole duty of keeping the brass polished. Now the fence no longer glitters in the sunlight; the ravages of time have made this piece of artwork quite dark, and passers-by speak of it as a "masterpiece in bronze." Flood died in Germany in 1891, and the mansion, acquired by the Pacific Union Club, was remodeled in 1910 by the well-known architects, Willis Polk and D. H. Burnham of Chicago. Today it is the only mansion of the bonanza group still standing.

Another house on Nob Hill opposite Stanford's was that of David Porter. This location was later acquired by James G. Fair and is now the site of the Fairmont Hotel. George Whittell and Robert Sherwood had their residences between Taylor and Jones streets on the south side of California Street. Near by was A. N. Towne's property. The Benchley cottage, purchased in the early days by E. B. Pond, was next to the Richard Tobin residence.

Other properties were owned in smaller parcels by Robert Hamilton, the Forman family, Lena H. Hill, and Sophie W. Sage.

Lloyd Tevis, lawyer, banker, and insurance broker, built on Taylor Street near Jackson an ornate structure, luxuriously furnished, containing great works of art. His neighbors were George Beaver, Senator George Hearst, Judge Hastings, Albert Miller, and James B. Haggin. Because of street boundary changes, the locations of their houses have been obscured.

The California Street cable-car patron never tired of comparing the dwellings lining the sides of the busy thoroughfare the line traversed. California Street was famous for the magnificent residences which housed the wealth, culture, and refinement of a growing metropolis. The homes had not only a distinctive individuality, in keeping with the influence and personality of their owners, but represented almost every stage of the city's striking growth. It was possible to see the change from the humble, square, four-walled abode clustered in the Western Addition to the more pretentious homes on the summit of Nob Hill. The exteriors were artistic, belonging to no one style of architecture but representing all the different orders in modified forms. Visitors from Eastern cities were impressed by the spacious grounds and well-kept lawns which surrounded the homes.

The California Street Cable Railroad Company rendered the Nob Hill dwellers and its patrons an efficient service worthy of the reputation of its incorporators. As the tracks stretched westward, men leveled the sand dunes and filled up the gulches, and where there had been only waste land, blocks of attractive residences appeared. In an easterly direction the cable cars became an increasingly important factor in penetrating the commercial and financial districts. The fire following the 1906 earthquake destroyed these residential palaces, the picturesque roofs with their towers, and the luxurious salons of almost priceless contents; and the Nob Hill of the 1880's became the exclusive hotel and apartment house district of the present day.

Chapter VII

CHINATOWN AND THE CABLE CARS

MUCH HAS been written about the early Chinese immigrants who contributed by their hard labor to the mining of gold and silver, the building of the transcontinental railroads, and the transformation of the sun-baked soil and river-soaked marshes of California into a land of waving wheat, blossoming orchards, and bumper potato crops. But not enough has been said of these humble toilers in many more ordinary walks of life—farm workers, cooks, and those dependable domestic servants generally known as houseboys. Without them it would have been difficult to maintain well-organized California communities and particularly a formal social life in San Francisco, a social life rivaling if not surpassing the traditional hospitality of the South.

Many of these unsung Oriental "faithfuls" of early San Francisco formed an important part of the California Street Cable Company's patronage. As the chief means of transportation between the palatial mansions on Nob Hill and the Chinese

Western terminus of the Market Street Cable Railway Company

Eastern terminus of the Geary Street Cable Railway

Quarter—which they proudly termed "The City of the Sons of Tang"—the California Street Line carried the bulk of the Chinese traffic.

The trip to Chinatown was an exhilarating feature of the long, steep descent from Nob Hill eastward toward the Bay. The gripman, when reaching the narrow, level strip of Dupont Street (now Grant Avenue), had to pull the brake handle with all his might to bring to a shivering stop the swiftly descending car in order to deposit his passengers at the gateway of Chinatown.

What delightful memories of the Chinatown of the 'eighties and 'nineties survive! Stretching north from red-bricked Old St. Mary's Cathedral to the slopes of Telegraph Hill, where the newly arrived Italian immigrants lived, lay Dupont Street, narrow, cobblestoned, cluttered with rambling two- and three-story buildings. The numerous balconies were strung with giant lanterns and huge signs, elaborately carved and gilded, and were decorated with large plants and bushes shaped to resemble the beasts and birds of the forest. Over the colorful, pagoda-like rooftops fluttered the weird dragon pennant of ancient China.

The Oriental Quarter of that period was squalid and unsanitary, but genuinely picturesque. It formed a city within a city, and comprised ten square blocks packed with humanity. It was crisscrossed with thoroughfares bearing such euphemistic names as "Street of the Sons of Tang," "Alley of the Imperial Consort of Heaven," "Avenue of Virtue and Harmony," and "Lane of the Golden Chrysanthemum."

Chinatown's fame as a sight-seeing attraction grew progressively. As a miniature reproduction of Canton—the City of the Rams, the native home of the original immigrants—its exotic atmosphere and its undeniable charm thrilled all comers, who viewed the unusual spectacle with wide-eyed amazement and pleasure. The sordidness and vulgarity of the commercialized vice fringing Chinatown's borders along with the unsavory

79

sights and sounds of the Barbary Coast were totally forgotten in the contemplation of the treasures from the Orient.

A thousand and one most interesting objects greeted the visitor's eye. Classical Chinese architecture displayed its strange peaked roofs, upturned eaves, latticed balconies, and tall, graceful columns, vividly colored. Flickering lanterns, red and green, adorned the alleys. Small shops, vending brocades, embroideries, curios, bronzes, jades, ivory, and coral carved in innumerable unusual designs, were numerous. These unique stores also displayed a large variety of fragile Canton chinaware. Native apothecaries stocked remedies compounded of everything natural to land, sea, or air. Chinese industry gathered around the cigar, shoe, and garment factories. Street peddlers and sidewalk merchants, with their pushcarts, baskets, and portable stands trimmed with brightly colored umbrellas and employing festive bunting as devices, attracted eager buyers of queer-looking Chinese cakes, candies, and nuts. Red Chinese bulletins several feet high inscribed with a maze of black, intricately fashioned, flowing Chinese calligraphy, containing news of importance, were pasted on the walls at prominent street corners. All these details contributed to the unrivaled character of Chinatown, which Charles Warren Stoddard in 1873 called "as rare a bit of old China as can be found without the Great Wall."

The Chinatown of those days, pulsating with life, was the center of the social and economic activities of all Chinese immigrants west of the Rockies. On commemorative occasions such as Chinese New Year, festivities often lasted more than a week. During this holiday season the New World was almost forgotten and these few blocks became a celestial city paying homage and deference to ancient rituals and customs. The Quarter would be magically transformed by the importation of forests of blossoming fruit-tree branches from the Santa Clara, Napa, San Joaquin, and Sacramento valleys. The air would become heavily laden with the fragrance of Chinese lilies, spicy foods, smoldering sandalwood candles on temple altars, and flaming incense before ancestral shrines. The noise of the machine-gun-like popping of knotted chains of firecrackers, often more than fifty feet in length, at times would shut out all other sounds. The sound of bronze gongs, the clashing of cymbals, and the shrill tones of native orchestras, preponderantly tympanic, would add to the hilarious excitement. The New Year's Good Luck Lion would prance and posture through the streets to the quaint rhythm of a giant kettledrum. The streets were always crowded with Chinese grown-ups in native costume, with an occasional child, dressed in gay silken attire, like a little idol, making a diminutive contribution to the colorful scene.

The cable cars became a positive barometer of social events in Chinatown. Heavy traffic of Chinese passengers indicated a Chinese feast or holiday. Scarcity or absence of Oriental riders, however, often meant another thing: Tong wars! These fierce internecine struggles between contesting factions constituted one of the banes of Chinese existence within the community. During these periodic clashes of opposing tongs, Chinese houseboys and laundrymen, even though noncombatants, would remain in hiding outside of the Quarter. During these feuds anyone near by was in danger of being killed by random shots and ricocheting crossfire from the narrow alleys. The flow of Chinese passenger traffic would not be resumed until the all-powerful Chinese Consolidated Benevolent Association, which constituted Chinatown's local self-government, announced that hostilities had ceased.

After weeks and months of tong warfare the declaration of peace would be signalized by heavy Chinese traffic. Then the appeal of Chinatown for the Chinese houseboys could not be gainsaid, for their social roots were grounded in the Quarter. It offered them news from home, books to read, special delicacies, "filles de joie," herbs to heal their ailments, and even Association hospitals in which to die. In sickness and in health, in business and in pleasure, their hearts' desires found fulfillment in Chinatown. Here life was sustained in a high and interesting tempo. Even the poorest houseboy found the opportunity to take a turn at fan-tan or to listen to native opera. When his money was gone he could still enjoy hours of interesting conversation with friends and kinsmen. It is not surprising, therefore, that after their day's work in other parts of the city many Chinese boarded the cable cars for their beloved Chinatown.

The cable cars were responsible for the development of many a strong inter-racial friendship. The crews of the cars soon came to know their Chinese passengers as they traveled daily back and forth. To the average San Franciscan of that period, all Chinese looked alike. Dressed in their clothes of shiny cloth, they presented an appearance which inspired a California wag to describe them as "polished" Chinese gentlemen. Their costumes, very often half-Chinese and half-Western, gave them a characteristic appearance. They had smooth-shaven faces, as well as shaven crowns, and jet black queues well oiled and intertwined with vermilion braid. Many of them wore black felt hats or bowlers, black cotton or silk jackets, American trousers, and black Chinese satin slippers with thick, white soles.

The crews of the cable cars learned to note the unusual qualities of these passengers of alien race. Despite their strange raiment and physical appearance, they found in them qualities, personal and social, which deserved approbation. A Chinese, for instance, never got drunk nor disturbed the peace. One never attempted to "beat" the conductor out of his fare. They took the early evening cars to Chinatown and the last ones back to their places of employment. Once their shyness was overcome, they were extremely friendly and very voluble in their pidgin English.

A gift-loving and gift-bearing race, the Chinese passengers were often generous in their presents to the streetcar men. If they won at the pie-gow or chuck-a-luck tables, they presented the conductors and gripmen with Chinese candies, objects of Oriental art, and occasionally a silver or gold piece. During the Chinese New Year period they would remember their cable-car friends with Chinese delicacies, bottles of whisky, and specially made frosted layer cakes. In view of this fraternization it was not strange that the Chinese passengers were popular with the cable-car crews. Quite regularly the last trip of the cars to the barns would witness the hegira of Chinese domestics hanging on to the running boards and shouting: "Aw-lai, Aw-lai! Now can go! Quickee, quickee sleep!"

Many momentous events have occurred in San Francisco's long years of existence. The earthquake and fire altered the appearance of the city radically and wrought vast changes in Chinatown. No longer is the Quarter physically or socially separated to the former extent from the major community. Chinatown has gone modern, has expanded.

The Quarter now embraces several blocks beyond the old "Street of the Sons of Tang"—Sacramento Street. Old St. Mary's still remains at the same location. But modern art goods shops, Japanese as well as Chinese, now stand side by side with exclusive American stores in the very heart of San Francisco's shopping district. And Sing Fat's, an internationally known landmark, with its several stories of exclusive Chinese art and wares, has disappeared, the ground floor becoming a Japanese bazaar and the upper stories a Japanese hotel.

The traveling public has made Chinatown one of the most popular sight-seeing spots in the country. Automobiles bearing license plates from every state in the Union are found parked in its streets and alleys. Native-born Chinese guides pilot the tourists through the Quarter, directing them to the modern stores, the curio shops, the temples and opera houses. When time and opportunity permit, visitors are shown the luxurious Americanized apartments, the newspaper offices, the Oriental cocktail bars with their Chinese barkeepers and girl crooners, their flaunting dragons, and their garish pagodas silhouetted against the low buildings—all flooded with multicolored neon illumination. Chinatown, exotically attractive, is the much-courted beautiful foster daughter of San Francisco.

However, this modernistic change leaves the crews of the cable cars strangely cold. Their intimate contacts with the Chinese houseboy passengers of yesteryear are no more. Their places have been taken by sophisticated American members of the younger Chinese generation, differing in but few respects from that of the community at large. Gone forever are the pigtails and black-garmented Chinese domestics and launderers who, flushed with the successes of fan-tan, used to shout goodnaturedly: "Hel-lo, Char-lee! You like 'um China candee? Me hab-bum heap goot luckee!"

The cable cars may still clatter and clang up their steep Nob Hill climb, but the riotous homeward journey of the Chinese domestics, formerly a unique midnight spectacle, is no more, although it remains vivid to many oldtimers.

CHAPTER VIII

JAMES B. STETSON
THE CABLE CAR COMES OF AGE

AFTER THE 1906 fire, cable operation on the Sutter Street Road gave way to electric power. The Pacific Avenue Line, conducted since 1887 as a branch of the Sutter Street, continued to operate by cable. Old-timers recall many prominent citizens who were regular patrons of the Pacific Avenue Cable Line, all of whom have passed away long ago. Among them should be mentioned Colonel Jonathan Drake Stevenson, who came to San Francisco in 1847 as commander of a volunteer regiment; William T. Coleman, leader of the committee of safety formed to rid the town of the lawless element; Charles Lathrop, brother-in-law of Leland Stanford, who lived on the northwest corner of Pacific and Van Ness avenues and who was quite popular among the platform men on account of his democratic ways.

Sentiment permitted the Pacific Avenue Line to continue long after it had ceased to be profitable and after the rolling stock, the track, and the street pavement had greatly deteriorated. Younger men had been substituted for the seasoned conductors. Families had moved away, and wooden dwellings of long standing yielded to the apartment house of the modern day. Newcomers, unacquainted with the tradition of the line, parked their automobiles in the street, bumper to bumper, causing much congestion. No longer did the cars stop in the middle of the block to receive and discharge passengers.

With the turn of the century, the California Street Cable Railroad Company, with James Stetson as its president, went through a trying period. A series of labor grievances not only taxed the patience of the management but swept down upon the whole city in quite the same manner as a plague.

In 1901 the teamsters' dispute confronted the community. During the strike there arose the necessity of replacing the Cable Company's wire rope. For after from one hundred sixty to one hundred eighty days, each cable in turn became stretched and worn and inefficient. It was always an interesting sight to watch the hauling of the cables from the California Wire and Rope Works, located in North Beach, to the powerhouse at Hyde and California streets. From forty to fifty horses were required to pull the two trucks which held the tremendous spool of coiled cable weighing many tons. Now in 1901 Stetson and Harris appealed to Mike Casey, president of the Teamsters Union, to supply the men and horses for the job, stating that his refusal would force them to stop operations. Nevertheless the request was refused. Stetson thereupon conceived the idea of sending to Stockton for one of the original Holt tractors, then available for special work. On an early Sunday morning the tractor conveyed its heavy burden along the Embarcadero, up Mission Street, and over to Taylor Street. A thousand people, mostly strikers and sympathizers, watched this unusual sight. On a slight climb on Taylor Street the tractor ran into difficulty. The burden was too heavy to haul over the rise, and Chief of

Police Whitman gave permission to make a detour to Van Ness Avenue and then over California Street to the carbarn. This concession was given in violation of a city ordinance, as no trucks, much less a Holt tractor, were permitted on the finest boulevard in the city. Whitman on that occasion took full responsibility upon himself and thereby helped the management to overcome a difficult situation.

At the beginning of 1906 San Francisco was enjoying a period of prosperity. Money was easy, prices were rising, and all soundly financed corporations were yielding satisfactory returns. The population trend continued to be favorable, and a brisk demand prevailed for real estate. Many houses were being constructed in the Western Addition. Automobiles had just come into use, and a dozen or so were to be seen on the city's streets. But travel on the cable cars was still increasing. The California Street Cable Railroad Company was paying excellent dividends, and its stock was selling at two hundred dollars a share on the San Francisco Stock and Bond Exchange.

On April 11, 1906, the directors of the company at their regular monthly meeting declared the usual monthly dividend of ninety cents a share payable next day. No further consideration was given to an offer, made in March by Adolph Spreckels, to buy control of the company at two hundred fifty-five dollars a share. Director Stetson favored selling out; but the Borel interests, which had the controlling power and influence, did not wish to give up an investment with so promising a future.

A week later came the greatest calamity in the history of San Francisco. An earthquake, followed by a great fire, terminated many of the city's pioneer industrial and financial institutions. The disaster of 1906 has been described in detail and historically recorded by many capable contemporaries. In this chapter reference will be made principally to the effect of the earthquake and fire on the California Street Cable Railroad Company.

California Street east of Powell, April 19, 1906

Powell Street Railway Company, Bay and Taylor streets, April 21, 1906

Eastern terminus of the Market Street Cable Railway, Oakland Ferries, 1890

Eastern terminus of the Market Street Railway Company,
Oakland Ferries, 1900

Cable Car Days in San Francisco

James Burgess Stetson, in his *Personal Recollections during the Eventful Days of April, 1906,* tells certain details of unusual interest, relying upon notes he had made while the happenings were fresh in his mind. On Wednesday morning, April 18, Stetson wrote:

I went over to the power house of the California Street Railroad and found that about seventy feet of the smoke-stack had fallen diagonally across the roof and about six feet of it into the stable, where there were two horses; fortunately, it did not touch them . . . . Things were considerably disturbed, but the engines were apparently uninjured. The watchman was not hurt, although bricks and mortar had fallen all around him. I was told that the water supply was stopped, and later learned that to be a fact, because the earthquake had broken the water mains.

The Spring Valley Water Company's mains had been broken by the earthquake; the threat of fire, with no water available, prompted Stetson to investigate. The following is a picture of what he found:

Early in the morning [Thursday] I went over to the California Street power-house and had a talk with Superintendent Harris. He said that he had run out twenty cars, but as the water was shut off and very low in the boilers, it was not safe to get up steam, and he was unable to get horses to haul the cars; so nothing could be done but await the result, which was that every car in the house and those on the street, some of them eight blocks away—fifty-two in all—were burned except one.

The next day Stetson went over to the California Street engine house, and found it in ruins. He wrote:

Beams, pipes, iron columns, tie-rods, car-trucks, and a tangled mess of ironwork, bricks, mortar, ashes, and debris of every description filled the place. The interior was unbearably hot, but I crawled into it through what was left of the front stairway, which was nearly filled with loose bricks, and the stone facings of the Hyde Street front. It was a sad sight affecting me greatly, for I had something to do with the construction of the plant from its inception. Seemingly everything was there, but rods, cranks, beams and pipes were out of shape and badly damaged, whether beyond hope of restoration I could not tell. No one was there or on the street, and I came away filled with anxiety. I had some hope, but whether the loss would be total or partial I could not say. A further examination showed more damage—one shaft fourteen inches in diameter was considerably bent out of line; some of the large sheaves were badly twisted. The exposed portion of a new cable coiled on a reel ready for use was so badly burned as to render the whole useless. . . . . The tank, encased in brick, contained 6,000 gallons of fuel oil, and with its contents was intact. The granite blocks on which the engines and drivers rested were badly cracked by the heat, and in some places entirely destroyed. Portions of the cables in use in the engine-room were ruined and on the street were burned off in several places. The prospect of ever repairing and getting the machinery and appliances in operation again seemed impossible.

At this time, about 8 A.M. Friday, I saw by the smoke that three large fires were burning at North Beach, spreading in the direction towards the Union Street engine house . . . .

I afterwards walked down into the business part of the city. The streets were filled with debris—in some places on Kearny and Montgomery Streets to the height of four feet and more. The tracks and slot rail of the California Street line were badly bent and twisted in many places. The pavement in numberless locations was cracked and warped. Few people were to be seen among the ruins, which added to the general gloom and desolation. I found it very difficult to orient myself when wandering not only in the ruins but also later in the rebuilt district, as all the old landmarks were gone. As there were no street cars running, I found my automobile extremely useful, although the rough streets filled with all sorts of debris, punctured the tires all too frequently.

On the Saturday after the fire the first meeting of the company was held at the home of John C. Coleman, on the corner of California and Franklin streets. It was difficult to find the directors; but Meyer, Coleman, Whittier, Borel, Stetson, and Harris were present. They were a bewildered and dejected group as they appraised the tremendous destruction of property values: How much is the loss of the California Street Cable Railroad Company? Will the stockholders be assessed? Is the

Sutter Street Railroad Company, Larkin Street branch;
Market at Ninth Street

Ferries and Cliff House Steam Line, 1888–1905

company bankrupt? Will the cable cars ever be able to operate again? Has San Francisco a future? The answers to all these questions were left in doubt. A committee was formed and instructed to report promptly on the damage done and the advisability and possibility of reconstruction.

In June the committee submitted its findings. After a lengthy discussion, it was determined by a unanimous vote to rehabilitate the road. Everything was left to Harris. Two months later restoration on a moderate scale had been accomplished. The first four cars were put in service with only a priming coat of paint, so anxious were the directors to resume operations.

True, old San Francisco was in ruins; but a new city was rising to become the monument to the enterprise of the inhabitants. Of course, certain old landmarks could not be replaced, but except for cracked-wall facings and displaced plaster the city's few modern steel structures had not been greatly injured. And the twofold visitation by fire and earthquake proved a blessing in some respects—San Francisco was given the great opportunity to rebuild upon a basis of permanence and beauty.

The financial, wholesale, retail, and shopping districts had been completely razed. The most densely populated areas east of Van Ness Avenue and south of Market and Mission streets were destroyed. In several spots on Van Ness Avenue the flames had leaped across that 125-foot thoroughfare and done some damage. Over twenty-eight thousand buildings were ruined, and the value of the property demolished ran up to $440,000,000, making the conflagration loss the greatest the world had ever known. From 5:15 A.M. on April 18 to 3:00 P.M. on the twentieth, some sixty hours, property was laid waste at the rate of over $7,000,000 an hour.

The greater part of the calamity was caused by the fire. For miles nothing inflammable remained standing. Bricks, stone, broken crockery, twisted iron and other metals, and charred telegraph and telephone poles were the only remnants. The loss of life was estimated at about four hundred fifty.

Many earthquake shocks were felt during the three days of the calamity, and for two months thereafter frequent tremors disturbed the community. John McGaw, the veteran realtor, wrote:

On Russian Hill, our house was the last dwelling to go. My father-in-law's residence on Jones Street was one of the houses that withstood the fire in that large area. The structure would have gone if I had not torn down all the window shades, curtains and drapes. Saturday morning, I went to the ruins of the Livermore house, situated on the peak of Russian Hill. I looked down upon desolation. There was no human being in sight. The area resembled a map; the streets were well defined; although I could not recognize any landmarks, for only the chimneys remained where houses formerly stood. At seven o'clock Saturday morning, the fire had burnt itself out and the battle was won.

Probably no Board of Directors' meeting of the California Street Cable Railroad Company was more dramatic than the one held in July 1906. The company had carried all its insurance with the Fireman's Fund Insurance Company. On the other hand, Fireman's Fund was a substantial stockholder in the California Street Cable Company. At the meeting sat John C. Coleman, a director and a prominent stockholder in both companies. Because of his position and influence, the other directors of the cable system had become stockholders in the insurance firm. A desperate situation had arisen, as both companies were financially impaired.

W. J. Dutton, president of the Fireman's Fund Insurance Company, had been invited to present the case of his concern. In simple words, with dignity, and with a sincerity and earnestness that won the admiration of the listeners, Dutton pictured the extent of the catastrophe as it affected his company. He described the company's gradual and extraordinary growth over a span of forty years, which by 1905 had brought it to the pinnacle of its success, commanding and enjoying the confidence of the insurance world. Only a few days ahead of April 18 the Fireman's Fund had declared its quarterly dividend; now that the company owed over $11,200,000 for fire losses in San Francisco alone, this dividend declaration had to be rescinded.

The men present knew the true meaning of the chaos produced by a catastrophe that had resulted in the separation of families, the rupture of business relations, the destruction of business ledgers, and the loss of contacts between merchant, banker, broker, and doctor and customers, clients, and patients. They had seen the interruption of gas and water service and the general accompanying disorganization. They had lived in camps with their fellow citizens through some of these momentous days.

The appeal of W. J. Dutton and his explanation of the financial condition of the company resulted in a resolution prepared and offered by J. Henry Meyer as follows:

Resolved, the California Street Cable Company compromise at fifty percent its losses on policies carried with the Fireman's Fund Insurance Company, and leave in abeyance for the present the acceptance or rejection of the stock offer made in addition to the cash settlement.

The resolution was duly seconded by A. H. Payson and unanimously carried.

The report of Engineer Stut, representing the streetcar company, and Adjuster Neilsen, representing the insurance company, indicated a property valuation involving approximately $285,000, on which the estimated fire loss amounted to $177,000. A cash award of $87,726 was accordingly made by the Fireman's Fund Insurance Company and accepted by the California Street Cable Railroad Company directors. The amount thus received from the insurance company and an additional $40,000 was constituted a rehabilitation fund.

Rapid reconstruction soon transformed the tangled mass of girders, beams, pipes, car trucks, iron columns, and brick and mortar into a new powerhouse on the site of the old plant.

95

Cable Car Days in San Francisco

During the first five weeks after the earthquake water had to be hauled in barrels from a great distance, and this slowed up construction. And building materials required for the foundation work were obtained only after many delays.

It is to be recalled that the main drive shaft in the powerhouse had been warped. Stetson conceived the idea of heating it and straightening it slowly. His method worked well, and the warped shaft was put into proper alignment. Stetson's ingenuity in such matters saved the stockholders large amounts of money and put the system back into operation by August 1906.

In the long history of the company, the first threat of a strike by the platform men came to the attention of the directors on August 28, 1906, when they received written demands from President Richard Cornelius of the Amalgamated Association of Street and Electric Railroad Employees of America. Stetson, when notified of the grievances, namely, the request for three dollars a day and an eight-hour day for platform men, presented the demands to the California Street Cable Railroad Company's directorate.

President Patrick Calhoun of the United Railroads, whose company already was strike-bound, acted fearlessly. Determined to break the strike, he resorted to the expensive method of employing James Farley to recruit a trainload of men from the great Eastern cities to serve as strikebreakers.

The Geary Street, Park and Ocean, and California Street lines were permitted to operate under the conditions that had caused the strike on the United Railroads. But the request for an increase in wages was repeated several times from August 1906 to April 1907. Finally, the men voted to strike on the California Street Cable Line, and the system suspended operations on April 27, 1907.

Stetson answered the union demands by stating:

The company was hard hit, only fifty cents on the dollar was received on our fire insurance. To replace the Jones Street cable line it will cost $20,000. We are not in a position to meet your request. Furthermore, we require trained men to operate the California Street cars. The United Railroads can get along, they say, without old hands, but we cannot break in new men readily, and we should not like to lose our old employees.

Stetson's appeal fell on deaf ears, and the management had to grant an increase in pay of two cents an hour in order to terminate the strike.

During the time the road was not operating because of the labor dispute, rehabilitation work continued. The rails between Drumm and Sansome streets had been depressed as much as sixteen inches in some places, and the earthquake had badly damaged the slot, requiring extensive and costly repairs.

By July 1908, twenty-seven months after the destruction of the powerhouse and the rolling stock, the road was restored to its previous first-class condition. Many changes had taken place in the resettlement of the city and by the opening of new districts. These had a direct effect upon the revenues of the cable system. Contrary to former experience, the income of the California Street section was now larger than that of the Hyde Street Line. In the six following years, the company's annual earnings increased steadily, and the stockholders had every reason to be satisfied. At the same time the patrons of the line were receiving excellent service.

Upon the death of James B. Stetson on August 21, 1909, J. Henry Meyer became president of the California Street Cable Railroad Company. He served in that capacity to 1921. Born in Nevada City, California, on March 24, 1855, Meyer had received his education in Geneva, Switzerland. Antoine Borel, ever on the lookout for capable young men for his flourishing banking institution, had taken Meyer into his establishment; before long the latter had become an outstanding figure in San Francisco's financial world. He served as a director of several prominent Western corporations, such as the California Street

Cable Railroad Company, the Wells Fargo Bank and Trust Company, the California-Oregon Power Company, the Spring Valley Water Company, and Golden State Milk Products Company, the predecessor of Golden State Company, Ltd. After Meyer's death, his son-in-law, Frank Buck, was elected to the Board of Directors of the California Street Cable Railroad Company.

John C. Coleman was another of the pioneers of San Francisco who was affiliated with this streetcar company almost from its inception. He was born in Walton, Suffolk County, England, and had come to California at the time of the discovery of gold. He and his brother, Edward Coleman, who came to the Golden State several years later, became identified with the gold-mining industry and opened the Morning Star Mine at Iowa Hill and the Idaho Mine in Grass Valley in 1867. Coleman was the first president of the narrow gauge railroad which ran from Colfax to Nevada City. He moved to San Francisco in 1893 and became active in the development of public utilities. He was a director of the Pacific Rolling Mills and vice-president for many years of the Fireman's Fund Insurance Company. John C. Coleman died March 23, 1919, at the age of ninety-five years. His son, S. Waldo Coleman, succeeded him on the Board of Directors.

A few years prior to Coleman's death, in 1915, the Cable Company created a new funded debt of $384,000, the successful placement of which was undertaken by the Anglo-London-Paris National Bank and the brokerage firm of J. Barth & Company. With the proceeds, President Harris refunded the bonds which had been outstanding since 1890. The affairs of the company continued to prosper so well that by 1928 the new issue was retired from the company's earnings.

Quite a number of changes in the personnel of the directors took place between 1915 and 1921. Antoine Borel was succeeded by John Freuler. J. Henry Meyer & Company succeeded the Borel firm as treasurer, continuing in this capacity until December 1, 1921, when that office was transferred to the Security Bank & Trust Company. The Wells Fargo Bank and Trust Company took over the treasurership of the Cable Company in 1924 and holds it to the present day.

The first threat of municipal ownership appeared on April 30, 1913, when James Rolph, Jr., was mayor of San Francisco. The Board of Supervisors passed a resolution requesting an offer from the California Street Cable Railroad Company to sell out to the City of San Francisco. The directors were given until June 2 to submit their proposition. The creation of the Municipal Railway of San Francisco had been approved; but, as municipal ownership was an untried undertaking in San Francisco and as the California Street Cable Railroad Company was a very lucrative enterprise enjoying exceptionally good management and an increasing daily traffic, the directors, in view of the excellent prospects for the road, felt justified in not entertaining the city's proposal. On the other hand, the Presidio and Ferries Railroad Company, because of the expiration of its franchise at about that time, had to sell out to the city.

On August 31, 1925, the Supervisors took up the municipal-ownership subject again and passed a resolution to acquire the eleven miles of track and the physical assets of the California Street Cable Railroad Company at the lowest price obtainable upon the expiration of its franchise in 1929. Negotiations were commenced on March 5, 1926, with a letter to the company written by John W. Rogers, then Clerk of the Public Utilities Committee, wherein he asked that a price be submitted at which the company would sell its property to the city. President Harris replied that his concern would rely on the justice and skill of the city engineers in appraising it, whereupon the valuation could be submitted to the stockholders for ratification. When the Supervisors took the stand that the company should appraise its property and then submit the valuation to the City Engineer's office for approval, Harris reiterated his faith in the fairness of City Engineer M. M. O'Shaughnessey and Nelson A. Eckart, his assistant. "Moreover," he said, "the franchise has four years more to run, and in view of the existing relations with the city authorities there seems to be no urgent necessity to take any action." In view of the foregoing it is quite significant that in 1929 the company obtained a twenty-five-year extension of its franchise privileges.

The death knell of the Pacific Avenue Cable Road rang when in the 1920's an aroused public condemned the line which had so long served the Pacific Heights district. Many residents who had grown up on the line and fought for places on the "front of the dummy" will yet miss the noises, rattles, and clanging bells, and the friendly conductors and gripmen, who knew the regular patrons by name and waited for them if they were not at the curb when the car came along. For with an impressive ceremony the last car was at length run into the barn, and in June 1929 the tracks were torn up and Pacific Avenue became one of San Francisco's busy automobile thoroughfares.

Chapter IX

JAMES W. HARRIS

THE CABLE CAR REACHES MATURITY

THERE STANDS on the southwest corner of California and Hyde streets a two-story, out-of-date, wooden building. The old-fashioned bay windows command an excellent view of the busy intersection. From the basement rises the monotonous hum of drive shafts, wheels, and motors. From the slots in the middle of Hyde and California streets emanates the song of the cables, suggesting the pulse beat of a metropolis. This building, which was reconstructed after the fire, is divided into two parts. The wooden portion houses the California Street Cable Railroad Company's executive offices. The brick structure houses its cars and the power plant for its cables. The interior of the building has remained virtually unchanged since 1906. Groups of blue-uniformed conductors and gripmen, waiting to relieve platform men on duty, are often found standing around the entrance.

On the second floor one finds a dark office on the door of

which is inscribed the word "President." Here, facing the window, sits an aging man. When one approaches him he has probably just completed the sale of a book of school tickets and is waving a bewildered child out of the office. A sparkle is in his eyes and a kindly smile plays about his lips as he remarks: "The selling of weekly tickets to school kids is one of the functions of the president of this company."

From his out-of-date desk with its crowded pigeonholes and with papers relating to pending business piled on its top, President Harris is able to look down on the cable crossing, from which, for over half a century, the cars have kept moving over the hills. He is the one man who, because of his close connection with the company since its inception, is in an excellent position to discuss its history. He is probably the only living man who has been affiliated uninterruptedly for sixty years with the same streetcar company.

Harris tells the following story:

I was born at Pictou, Nova Scotia, on December 28, 1854. There were nine children in our family. I left my place of birth for the United States when I was seventeen years old, worked for a while in Massachusetts, Rhode Island, Illinois, and then moved on to California, the land of unlimited opportunities.

The train took eleven days to cross the continent. The trip over the prairies, at twenty-five miles an hour, was rough, dusty and monotonous. George Pullman's new palaces on wheels were operating in the East, but only day coaches were supplied to Western travel. At night I would adjust the seat in an attempt to secure some comfort and sleep. A considerable part of the food I needed on the journey I took with me. A stove in the car was used to prepare some simple dishes and to make coffee. There were frequent shifts along the line, as there were several independent railroads interconnecting; engines had to be changed, and delays were the rule rather than the exception.

Somewhere in Utah our progress was blocked by a landslide. The conductor informed us that it would be days before a train could pass. I had the alternative of either returning with the train to the last station or walking ahead three miles to where the conductor could telegraph for an "extra" to take us on. I decided to walk ahead, and shall never forget that adventure. The rain poured down pitilessly, and fitful gusts of wind drove sheets of water into our faces. Our feet sank deep into the mud, and we had to push through brush and wade shallow streams before we finally arrived at the next depot, which was nothing but a slab shanty. The only sign of life was a scraggy, half-drowned chicken wandering aimlessly about. After a while a woman appeared wearing a calico bonnet and holding her scanty skirts. She was willing enough to make us comfortable; but not a mouthful of anything in the way of food, not even a cracker, was to be had, and we saw the dinner hour come and go, in a state of melancholy depression. After six hours of waiting an "extra" arrived and we resumed our journey. The eager discussion of this last adventure drew us closer together, leading to a pleasant companionship among the passengers, who turned out to be quite a congenial lot. I was then about twenty years old, but looked rather mature for my age. Of course I was a total stranger in the West, and while I had a sister living in San Francisco I did not even know her address.

As we neared our destination, a fellow came through the train offering information and assistance. He introduced himself as a Wells Fargo agent, and he looked the part—tall, strong, and of the true Western type. Prefacing his statements with the remark that he was not allowed to do any soliciting, he emphatically recommended the American Exchange as the best place at which to put up. Whether Wells Fargo and Company had an interest in that particular hostelry or the hotel gave the agent a commission for drumming up business, I never knew nor cared. Those were the days when the hotels had their horse carriages at the Broadway Depot and the driver with the loudest voice had the best chance at the business.

My first impression of San Francisco was favorable, and I remember quite distinctly saying to a young fellow who traveled with me: "Here is where I am going to stay." And I made a resolution then and there to make good in this promising community.

San Francisco was a young city; everything looked new; everybody seemed to have something to do—life was free. The town was renowned for men of wealth and accomplishment and for its beautiful women. It was the westernmost outpost of civilization, and the heart of the West.

My interest in cable cars began when I first saw a little vehicle tugging its way up the Clay Street hill without being pushed or pulled

Western terminus Sutter Street branch, United Railroad, 1900

Market Street Railway Company mail car, 1888

by any visible mechanism. I shall never forget the thrill of seeing the car moving along without any engine or horse propelling it.

I had hardly any money left, but easily secured my first job, which paid me a few dollars a day. For eighteen months I was employed at a quicksilver mine in Lake County, at an unattractive, barren, God-forsaken place. When the carpentry work for which I was hired was completed, I was overjoyed to return to San Francisco and determined to be more discriminating in the future as to the jobs I would accept.

My next employment was with James B. Haggin and Lloyd Tevis in Kern County on a 90,000-acre ranch. While working there I made one of my periodic trips to make purchases at a grocery store in one of the communities near by. There I was confronted with the spectacle of five Mexicans being hanged in a courtyard. I shall never forget that gruesome sight. Their offense was horse stealing, which had become so commonplace that law-abiding men had to take justice in their own hands.

A short time later I heard of a job and was advised to call regarding it on Henry Root in the three-story brick building on the corner of Fourth and Townsend streets. This building housed the offices of the Central Pacific Railroad Company. Henry Root was connected with the Pacific Improvement Company, a construction subsidiary of the Central Pacific. He engaged me as a carpenter with the California Street Railroad at $2.50 a day. The Pacific Improvement Company had constructed the cable system for Leland Stanford. I started to work in April 1879. In 1884 the line was extended from Fillmore Street to Presidio Avenue. The date was approximately a year after the company had begun operations. It was my duty to repair the cars. I soon became shop foreman and later master mechanic. In 1889 I had charge of the extension work along Hyde, Jones, and O'Farrell streets and also of the extension from Kearny to Drumm Street, where S. H. Holmes was employed as engineer. In 1909 I became vice-president and general manager and was given a place on the Board of Directors. Upon the death of J. Henry Meyer in 1922 I was elected to succeed him as president and also retained my former title of General Manager.

Previous to my taking charge of the road, our cables were purchased from various companies, including Roebling's and some English and German concerns. I came to the conclusion that it would be more satisfactory to have the cables made locally, although the price might be somewhat higher. The California Wire Works, with whom Hallidie was connected, was in a position to meet our needs.

In the early days of the California Street Cable Railroad Company, I became acquainted with Governor Leland Stanford, whom, of course, I had known by reputation. I can remember his silk hat, his gold cane, his long-tailed coat, low vest, black tie, and turned-down collar. He was a large burly man with a ruddy complexion, and his gray-blue eyes were deep-set. He spoke with a low and melodious voice. He enjoyed a high degree of popularity, which was well deserved because of his vigorous and resourceful character. On the street when they met the "old man," all who knew him would take off their hats, and the Governor would courteously return the salutation. He was credited with being the father of the Republican Party in California. Before coming to the Coast, he practiced law in Wisconsin and this qualification and experience was of great value to him in many ways in his subsequent career. It is a mistaken idea that Leland Stanford's influence rested wholly on his wealth. He was a born leader and made his influence felt in every community where he lived. The private life of this pioneer was simplicity itself. He was slow spoken, direct and earnest in conversation, and religious at heart. His educational ideals were inspired by a conception of teaching and training for usefulness in life.

One of the best stories I heard Leland Stanford tell was during the gay 'nineties when gentlemen wore expensive diamond and pearl studs in their shirt fronts. In later days, the diamond studs were worn only by gamblers and saloon men. When Charles Crocker returned from his European trip, he showed his friends his pearl studs bought in Paris. He was proud of them and showed them to the Governor.

"Rather expensive?" asked Stanford.

"Yes, but I like them," replied Crocker.

Next day when the two met at a directors' meeting, the Governor asked Crocker to see him for a moment.

"Charlie, what do you think of my pearl studs?" asked Stanford.

"My golly! they are beautiful. Really, they are better than mine. Where did you get them?"

"Oh, well, I bought them in San Francisco."

"Rather expensive?"

The Governor chuckled: "Charlie, I discovered them in a store on Market Street. I gave the man three dollars for them."

James W. Harris

I recall another prank played by Stanford of which Crocker was the target. In those days these two bosom friends would drive their fast horses through Golden Gate Park with such speed that one day a park policeman lost his patience and stopped Stanford to remonstrate with him. The Governor was always suave and pleasant.

"Officer, you are right," he said; "but don't stop me this time. Charles Crocker is right behind me going just as fast as myself, pinch him instead of me."

Whereupon, with a smile, he lightly tapped his animal with the reins and the horse raced away. Looking back he saw that Crocker had been stopped by the same policeman, as had been suggested.

The earthquake marked the passing of the time-honored institution of the livery stable, which was in some respects the prototype of today's garage. A good part of the livery stable's income was derived from the Sunday buggy rides through Golden Gate Park to the Cliff House. When the horses were returned on Sunday night, the stable-keeper never failed to make the same comment: "You've druv this hoss purty hard, young man." In those days it required no license to drive a horse, and almost every male knew how to handle the ribbons. Patient Dobbin in his time served his task faithfully, and today when one sees a "nag" carrying on instead of being in the pasture to enjoy his few remaining years, one might be reminded of those bygone days when the prominent Nob Hill dwellers considered it important to maintain their own stables.

From this bay window overlooking California Street I have observed the different ways women use to stop the cable cars. Their attitudes and facial expressions are characteristic and seem to offer a clue to their individuality. For example, there is a severe, long-faced, old-maid type. She raises her arm almost as soon as she can distinguish the figure of a gripman and with her forefinger takes deadly aim at his eyes. The workings of her mind are written all over her face. Her countenance speaks, saying, "Pass me at your peril." The fear that a car may not stop is latent in the majority of women's minds. This accounts for their extraordinary earnestness and energy in halting it. They frequently overlook the fact that the management has a service to perform and depends upon its patrons' fares to pay wages. Some women gesticulate with both arms, much as if they were signaling a locomotive to prevent an accident. Anxiety is registered all over their faces. When the car stops they probably feel convinced that a single

James W. Harris, with cable-car grips

Market Street Railway Company, Powell and Market streets, 1942

gesture less on their part would have failed to bring it to a halt. The fact that the gripman is employed for the purpose to stop for passengers, and is particularly instructed to do so, apparently does not enter their minds. Very often young and pretty women who have faith in the power of their personal appeal merely incline their heads gracefully toward the gripman, certain that he and all the world are eager to serve them. There is also the humble woman, with her baskets and bundles. She knows by reason of her parcels that she will be unwelcome to passengers and conductor, and the knowledge makes her shy or defiant in proportion to the sweetness or bitterness of her nature.

During the years that I have been connected with the company I have trained myself to give careful attention to the details of my work. As a mechanic in the company's shop I gathered a great deal of experience which later proved valuable to me as superintendent. Many and varied were the episodes I witnessed.

One of them, which I particularly like to relate, happened one morning in connection with my difficulty in opening the office safe. I was compelled to send for an expert locksmith. He came and tried the combination, but for some reason it did not release the bolts of the lock. He listened to the sounds made in turning the dial, and as he could not get satisfactorily by ear the sounds that he wanted, he placed one end of a straight-grained piece of wood between his teeth and rested the other end on the rim of a disk containing the dial. By this means the sounds were conducted to his brain, enabling him to make the mechanism click; and, presto, the lock yielded and the safe was opened. The operation took about twenty minutes. I asked him what his charge was, and he told me it amounted to fifteen dollars.

I pointed out that it took him only twenty minutes to do the work and that forty minutes would cover the time of the absence from his shop and insisted that he render me an itemized bill. The safe-opener complied with my request, and this was his bill:

Cable carfare to and from shop	$ .10
Time absent—40 minutes	1.00
Knowing how	13.90
	$15.00

I appreciated the force of logic contained in the last item and paid the bill without further comment.

Cable Car Days in San Francisco

I have always enjoyed good relations with our platform men. For the past fifty-two years I have conscientiously endeavored to be fair in my dealings with them and helpful to our employees whenever I could. Perhaps the confidence the men had in me was a contributing factor inducing the Market Street Railway people to make me an offer to work for them. That was in 1902, when Charles Holbrook was president. Their strike had just been settled, and the management wanted me as superintendent. The offer did not attract me because I was satisfied where I was. In 1913 I was invited by Supervisors Vogelsang and Hayden to accept the superintendency of the Municipal Railway. Although I had the assurance of the fullest confidence of Mayor James Rolph, Jr., the Board of Supervisors, and the Department of Public Works, I could not persuade myself to make a change. The California Street Cable Railroad Company was my pet, and no other system could have the same appeal.

I remember the consolidation of the principal railways of the city in 1893. At that time it appeared as if too much capital stock had been issued for the various lines. The Market Street Railway people received $13,500,000 in shares for their system, the Omnibus Company $3,000,000 for their property, and the Ferries and Cliff House owners $1,500,000 for their franchise, rolling stock, and real estate. With that amalgamation, the Market Street Cable Company, Market and Fairmont, Park and Ocean, Potrero and Bayview, Southern Heights and Visitacion Valley, City Railway Company, Central Railway Company, Omnibus Railway, North Beach and Mission, and Ferries and Cliff House systems ceased to exist. In 1902 the United Railroads took over the operation of the Market Street, Sutter, Sutro, and San Mateo Lines.

In 1907 the Market Street Railway Company, under the presidency of Patrick Calhoun, acquired one thousand shares of the California Street Cable Company's capital stock. The shares were purchased from the Fireman's Fund Insurance Company, with the intention of eliminating further competition. These plans were changed subsequently and the investment was liquidated in 1917. This abandonment was ill-advised, when one considers the excellent earnings of the California Street Cable Railroad Company through the years. The record of the profits under Stanford's stewardship is not available, but it is a known fact that the investment was a lucrative one. Up to 1940 the company had paid approximately six hundred dollars a share in dividends upon the original per share investment of sixty dollars. In addition, the earnings were sufficient to replace the rails in 1908, to retire $960,000 of the First Mortgage Six Per Cent Bonds which were issued to finance the construction of the Hyde Street Line, to build a new power plant, and to defray the cost of the extension from Kearny Street to Drumm Street—all this on the basis of the five-cent fare which was instituted over sixty-five years ago. The policy of the company is to maintain this five-cent fare upon the twelve miles of track it now operates, in spite of the fact that seven and one-half cents is the average prevailing rate throughout the United States.

Furthermore, the properties, as carried on the books, have been written down to the maximum extent allowed by the California Railroad Commission and a high-grade investment portfolio has been accumulated through the years, available as a reserve against losses due to accidents and other unforeseen contingencies.

One must not overlook the rapid changes that are taking place in mass transportation. The recent improvement in streamlined trolley cars, the developments in the field of diesel power and super busses have been noteworthy. I hesitate to prophesy what the future holds for the remaining cable-car lines in San Francisco. The history of this company has been so closely interwoven with the growth of this city that its future arouses considerable interest with sentimental-minded citizens.

Mr. Harris finished. A satisfied smile conveyed the thought that he had nothing further to say. His eyes seemed to moisten a trifle as he turned in his chair and resumed reading the correspondence awaiting his attention.

CHAPTER X

FADING OUT

NO TRANSPORTATION system continues indefinitely. Despite their initial novelty and their decades of picturesque and efficient service, cable cars have almost disappeared from San Francisco streets. Just as John Wesley Shaw's cinder-belching steam paddy—a familiar sight after 1860, first occupied in filling in waterfront lots and then in drawing street cars on Market Street—at length became superfluous, so cable cars were beginning to be replaced by electrically propelled vehicles in the late 1880's and in our day surviving cable lines on the steepest hills are being displaced by motor coaches.

The phenomenal recovery achieved by San Francisco following the 1906 earthquake and fire prepared the way for subsequent engineering achievements such as the Panama Pacific International Exposition, tunnels, skyscrapers, and the San Francisco–Oakland Bay Bridge, the Golden Gate Bridge, Treasure Island, and the Golden Gate International Exposition. These and other modern developments inevitably affected transporta-

112

tion. The San Francisco Bay ferries have been largely discontinued. They could not compete with the San Francisco–Oakland Bridge. The Marin Ferry, instituted by Juan Reed in 1826 and taken over by William A. Richardson in 1836, was discontinued on February 28, 1941, outmoded by the Golden Gate span.

Of course the cable lines have been involved. When newspapers announced that the Castro Street Cable Line, a segment of the Market Street Railroad Company, was going to be abandoned, the public was given the last opportunity to ride on it before it passed into history. A few years after the Market Street Cable system commenced operating, the Castro Street Cable Line was built in 1887 and thereafter its white ivory cars ran from Market to Twenty-sixth Street. Three cars were operated on a leisurely schedule; on Sunday travel was light, and two cars sufficed to handle the riding public.

On that perfect spring day, April 6, 1941, the line appeared lonely and desolate. Only two cars were in operation. The week before a careless driver had run into the third cable car and permanently put it out of commission. For over half a century these ancient hill-climbers had been the most reliable form of transportation known for scaling the seventeen per cent grade on the Castro route. Originally the cars had operated on Market Street to the Ferry, but electric trolleys had supplanted them there after the fire in 1906. Plodding steadily along at an eight-mile-an-hour gait, one day after another, up one side of the street and down the other side, they were important to many riders. By 1941 the roadbed had become rough because repairs had been neglected.

In spite of the large notice, "No Talking with the Platform Men," both gripman and conductor were communicative. The former had once been a hack driver in San Francisco. He complained about the frequent and costly accidents which occurred despite the clanging gong which he vainly rang to coax motorists and pedestrians to yield the way. Perhaps in the passing of the years he had lost some of his skill in operating the two cumbersome hand-grips. The conductor had accepted his job thirty-six years before with the assurance of the superintendent that he could have it for life. Now new Diesel-propelled equipment had arrived on the scene and both he and his car were outmoded. So the last ride was taken.

All San Francisco was familiar with the Fillmore Street hill cable line which served as a cross-town extension of the Market Street Railroad Company. The cars operated by electric and cable power on a twenty-four per cent grade between Broadway tween Vallejo and Green streets. From Green to the north-tween Broadway and Green streets. From Green to the northern terminus, Marina Boulevard, however, the car operated by electric power only.

Few people realize the study given to the safety devices for the protection of the passengers. Their application in the operation of these cars was especially interesting. The car at the foot of the hill was connected with the grip by a drawbar, the grip being permanently fastened to a one and three-eighths-inch endless underground cable. A man stationed at Green Street handled the connection. The drawbar was heavy and was operated by a small air cylinder. The grip slipped into an automatic locking latch, the latch having a special locking key as an additional safety measure. It was impossible for the car at the top of the hill to start until the car at the bottom had been securely connected with the cable. When the grip at the bottom of the hill had been locked, the car at the top still could not move. When everything was in readiness, the operator at the foot of the hill signaled the inspector at the top by an electric bell. When the operator at the bottom received the return signal, he opened the lock in the slot which permitted the grip to pass. The operation of this lever also turned on a light at the top of the hill, indicating that the slot was clear. After the up-car had passed over the hills and the grip attached to the down-hill car had passed through the automatic locking slot, the Green Street man disconnected the down-car and it continued by electricity to the Marina Boulevard. Meanwhile the next upbound car took its place ready for the up-hill climb. Thus the car going down pulled the up-car up. At the end of the day the last car up was counterbalanced by a balance car, which remained at the bottom of the hill over night, ready to take the first car down in the morning.

This method of operation had been in use since 1915, succeeding a similar method with older equipment in use since 1890. The older equipment operated without air brakes, a gate in connection with folding steps making it impossible to board or leave a car until it had come to a stop and the gate had been opened. In 1944 nothing remains of this funicular-like arrangement except the memory; the rails and slot have been removed and the streets have been paved.

For some months in 1941 the rumor had circulated that the Clay Street Cable Line would be replaced by motor coaches. Many citizens who had accepted the cable car as a traditional part of San Francisco became indignant—the world's first cable line must not be scrapped. Newspapers expressed opposition to the move; and delegations appeared before the Board of Supervisors in protest. A "Save the Cable Car League" was formed by those who held dear those faithful hill-climbers. But the motives behind this were not unmixed, and the line was doomed.

No celebration was held on February 15, 1942, when, about midnight, the last Clay Street Cable run was made. Few of the five thousand "Save the Cable Car League" members braved the hour to witness this historic event. Only Mrs. Anna Mezquida, F. G. Will, Robert O'Brien, Gripman Erwin, and Conductor Riordan rode Car 26 along Sacramento, over Larkin, to Clay, down the long hill to Mason, and finally into the car shed. The car was then shuttled into a large elevator, taken to a second level, hitched to a small tractor, and pulled to a turntable.

Cable Car Days in San Francisco

"This is the end of the line!" shouted Gripman Erwin, taking off his gloves; and downstairs, in the stillness of his office, Superintendent Thomas wrote his last report for the Sacramento line, ending: "at 1:00 o'clock of February 16th the Sacramento cables were thrown clear of the winding machinery and left dead on the floor."

At this writing apparently no steps have been taken by San Francisco to acquire the last remaining privately operated property, that of the California Street Cable Company, though it has been offered for sale to the municipality. Perhaps this line will continue to serve San Francisco citizens and visitors, a remarkable carryover from a bygone age.

Cable cars still crawling over the brows of San Francisco hills represent for the period of their origin a mechanical achievement comparable with its most modern tunnels and bridges and provide a stimulus to future progress, greatness, and prosperity.

APPENDIX

HENRY CASEBOLT AND THE SUTTER STREET CABLE RAILROAD CO.

SAN FRANCISCO, CALIFORNIA
July 26, 1944

MR. EDGAR M. KAHN

DEAR MR. KAHN:

In the early 1860's, horse-drawn busses ran at irregular intervals along a few routes. The busses were small and uncomfortable. The fares were high; that from the City front to Woodward's Gardens was fifty cents on weekdays and one dollar on Sundays and holidays. To remedy this condition, several horse-drawn street-car lines were built along the downtown streets, some extending into the Mission District as far as Mission Dolores. These lines were built through the most populous portions of the City.

The most daring enterprise of this kind was undertaken in 1865 by some real-estate operators who bought up a large tract of land out in the sand hills along Sutter Street. They conceived the idea of building up the district by constructing a horsecar line on Sutter Street from Sansome to Larkin streets. Few streets had been laid out, and there were scarcely any dwellers in this district.

The promoters awarded the contract for building this road to Henry Casebolt. Under-financed, they hoped to sell lots fast enough to pay for the work as it progressed. The contract price was about $165,000. They were disappointed in their lot-selling campaign, and before the work was half finished Mr. Casebolt had to take stock in the company in payment for his work. By the time the rails reached Larkin Street he found himself with the railroad in his own hands.

The grade up to Leavenworth Street from both the eastern and western approaches was steep, and it was necessary for an extra team to assist the regular team in pulling the cars to that summit. Mr. Casebolt used a team of hill horses for that purpose on the east side. People who had built homes in that neighborhood sued Mr. Casebolt and obtained an injunction against him on the ground of cruelty to animals.

Cable Car Days in San Francisco

In time the people who lived on Clay Street hill, between Kearny and Leavenworth, required a means of getting to their homes. That was one of the most thickly settled districts in the City. The hills were too steep for busses or horsecars. Mr. Hallidie conceived the idea of building a street-car line where the cars were drawn up and down the hills by an endless cable. Thus the cable was born. The first trip was made August 1, 1873. One of the principal difficulties to be overcome was devising a mechanism to be attached to the cars whereby they could grasp the cable or release it. Mr. Hallidie's grip consisted of an upper and a lower plate to be clamped to the cable by a large screw. This screw was operated by the gripman spinning a glorified automobile-steering wheel.

After Mr. Casebolt had been operating for ten years, he decided on similar propulsion for his line. On January 27, 1877, his first cable car operated on Sutter Street from Sansome to Larkin Street; later its route was extended to Buchanan. The Woodward's Gardens branch line was likewise converted to cable from Sutter to the Mechanics' Institute Pavilion at Hayes Street, and the horse line operated from Hayes Street to the Gardens. In 1879 a further extension was completed on Sutter from Buchanan to Central Avenue (formerly Cemetery Avenue, now Presidio Avenue). The cable was operated from a powerhouse on the latter thoroughfare between Post and Sutter. This route superseded the preceding circuitous horsecar line and became exceedingly popular.

The Larkin Street line was extended across Market to Mission Street on Ninth at about the same time the Market Street Railroad was building its cable line down Market Street. Having been finished first, the Sutter Street cars were operated by cable across Market. When the Market Street Railway completed its system, it laid its cable above the Larkin Street rope, causing the latter cars to stop again at the Mechanics' Pavilion. The Sutter Street Company claimed that priority of operation entitled it to have its cable uppermost, whereas the Market Street Company based its claim for this advantage on priority of franchise. The controversy was finally decided by the Court in favor of the Market Street Railway Company, and the Sutter Street line had to reconstruct its crossing.

The Sutter Street line was the first to use the lever side grip. By this method the cable was fed from the side instead of from the bottom. This company was the first to use horizontal pulleys or drums on curves, permitting a grip to retain its hold while passing around such a curve. The grip was also free to swerve at "let go" and "pick up" points while the running track remained straight.

In 1883, after Robert Morrow *et al.* had assumed ownership, a new powerhouse was constructed on the southeast corner of Sutter and Polk streets, and the Larkin Street line turned into Post and up Polk, later displacing the horsecars over the latter streets to Pacific Avenue, thence out to Broderick. The older lines were reconstructed with permanent concrete conduits. The Larkin Street line extended down Ninth from Mission to Brannan, where an outlet was provided for future extension into the Potrero Hill district which, however, was never built.

By 1890 the Sutter Street Railroad found itself bottled up at the cemetery terminus, whereas its competitors furnished service with steam-dummy lines to Golden Gate Park and the California and Jackson Street lines enjoyed the additional traffic to the Cliff House over the scenic route via Land's End, which became exceedingly popular and known all over the country. This trip, however, required an extra nickel, which irked Adolph Sutro, who had acquired the original Land's End franchise but had transferred it to the Ferries and Cliff House Railroad without exacting a specific promise of a downtown transfer. Sutro then procured a new franchise from Geary, along Presidio Avenue, to California, and out over the existing No. 2 line, with a branch along Eighth Avenue to the Park. He was ready to deal with the Geary Street, Sutter Street, California Street, and Ferries and Cliff House railways for downtown transfers; but Robert Morrow was most desperately in need of extended service and made the deal with Sutro to the exclusion of the others, and when the Sutro Railroad electric service was inaugurated a transfer privilege to the Sutter Street lines and a five-cent fare downtown were effected. This created such a favorable reaction that Sutro was elected Mayor of San Francisco.

After the death of Sutro, his heirs proceeded to sell the Sutro Railroad. During the court proceedings James B. Stetson, President of the California Street Railroad, raised Morrow's bid for the property. The courtroom was immediately turned into an auction room. Morrow finally won out, and the Sutro and Sutter Street railroads became one.

Henry Casebolt started a blacksmith and horseshoeing shop, and developed it into a wagon and carriage factory. He was a contemporary and competitor of John Studebaker, founder of the family that has gone so far in the automobile industry. Mr. Casebolt had a shop at the southwest corner of Fifth and Market streets where Penney's store is now located, and he moved from there to the north side of Market Street below Montgomery—the present site of the Hobart Building. In the latter days of his activities with the Sutter Street road he built a factory at the northeast corner of Union and Laguna streets. Mr. Casebolt not only designed the balloon car but also built the Mission Street bobtail cars which ran to the Gardens.

His later inventions were brought about by compelling circumstances. The arrangement of the pulleys that carried the cable in the slot of the Clay Street road did not suit him, and he devised a new suspension of the cable. Hallidie had patented his screw-operated grip and demanded $50,000 royalty from the Sutter Street road for its use there. Instead, Mr. Casebolt invented the lever-operated grip, substantially the same as that used today on the surviving California Street line.

Mr. Casebolt's success brought him national fame and he received contracts in the building of cable roads in Chicago, Kansas City, Philadelphia, Cleveland, and St. Louis.

FABIUS T. FINCH

THE MARKET STREET CABLE RAILWAY COMPANY

SAN FRANCISCO, CALIFORNIA

MR. EDGAR M. KAHN   July 26, 1944

DEAR MR. KAHN:

When the ferry landings were transferred to the foot of Market Street from Broadway, every street railroad in San Francisco applied for a franchise down our main thoroughfare to connect with the new facilities.

The Market Street Railroad Company had already operated steam and horsecars to this point. Now the Omnibus Railroad Company secured an extension of its franchise on Market from Sansome to the ferries and from Second to Third Street, and paralleled the Market Street Railroad by laying its tracks alongside. Thus was born four-track operation on Market Street.

The North Beach and Mission Railroad franchise, permitting the operation of horsecars from the ferries to Pine Street, and the franchise given the Central Railroad to operate to Bush Street were subject to a city ordinance which limited operations of street-car companies with duplicated franchises to five consecutive blocks or less. The tracks of these lines connected with the outer track of the Omnibus Railroad Company. The Sutter Street Railroad had more difficulty in securing an extension of its Market Street franchise from Sansome to the ferries, as the Omnibus Company claimed the extension exceeded the five-block legal limit for joint use. After a court battle the Sutter Street Company secured a franchise which has survived all later attacks and is in effect today.

The promoters of the Ferries and Cliff House Railroad obtained a franchise to operate from the ferries over Clay to Battery, to Jackson, out the latter thoroughfare to First Avenue, Jackson, Steiner, Washington, Battery, and Sacramento streets to the ferries. They then acquired the Powell Street Railroad Company's franchise over that thoroughfare from Market Street to Bay Street but, finding the company involved in controversy with the Omnibus and N. B. & M. railroads on the north end of Powell, decided to divert the line over Jackson to Mason, to Montgomery (now Columbus Avenue), to Taylor, to Bay, and over the latter thoroughfare to the waterfront. This portion, however, was never built and operated as a cable line.

Their powerhouse was located at the northwest corner of Mason and Washington streets. The cable conduits were all brick, while other lines used concrete.

The Jackson Street line was diverted down Central (now Presidio) Avenue to California Street. They had acquired the Sutro franchise on California Street from First Avenue to the Cliff House, which they intended operating as a steam railway, and made a deal with the California Street Railroad by which they used the latter's franchise on California Street from Presidio to First Avenue, connecting the steam line with the cable roads terminating on California Street and Presidio Avenue. They also obtained a franchise over Seventh Avenue from California Street to Fulton Street, thus reaching Golden Gate Park; and transfers were issued to both Jackson and California Street cables, according to the agreement, while the Cliff House trains charged an extra nickel.

Later this company acquired the Clay Street Hill Railroad and extended it westbound on Sacramento to Walnut Street. Eastbound, the cars operated over Sacramento, Larkin, and Clay streets to the ferry.

When the Mid-Winter Fair was proposed in 1893, this cable line was extended out Sacramento and Lake streets to Sixth Avenue and Fulton Street. The cable operating this extension was that of the McAl-

121

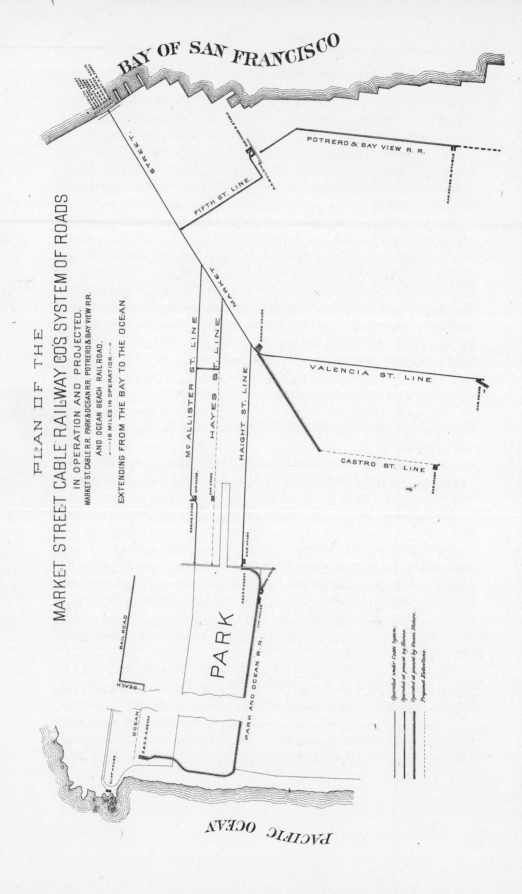

BAY OF SAN FRANCISCO

PLAN OF THE

MARKET STREET CABLE RAILWAY CO'S SYSTEM OF ROADS

IN OPERATION AND PROJECTED.

MARKET ST. CABLE R.R. PARK & OCEAN R.R. POTRERO & BAY VIEW R.R.

AND OCEAN BEACH RAIL ROAD.

←— 18 MILES IN OPERATION. —→

EXTENDING FROM THE BAY TO THE OCEAN.

POTRERO & BAY VIEW R. R.

CAR HOUSE & STABLE

FIFTH ST. LINE

MARKET STREET

ENGINE HOUSE

VALENCIA ST. LINE

CAR HOUSE

McALLISTER ST. LINE

HAYES ST. LINE

HAIGHT ST. LINE

ENGINE HOUSE

CAR HOUSE

CASTRO ST. LINE

CAR HOUSE

CAR HOUSE

PARK

PASS. R.R. DEPOT

CAR HOUSE

PARK AND OCEAN R. R.

BEACH RAIL ROAD

OCEAN

PASS. R.R. DEPOT

CLIFF HOUSE

Operated under Cable System.

Operated at present by Horses.

Operated at present by Steam Motors.

Proposed Extentions.

PACIFIC OCEAN

lister Street line, which had been extended to Eleventh Avenue. The steam line on Seventh Avenue was abandoned; but the little waiting room in the Park opposite Seventh Avenue still bears the sign of the Powell Street Railroad Company.

Around 1880 the control of several of the important horsecar lines was acquired by individuals acting for Leland Stanford and Charles F. Crocker. On February 23, 1883, these men of wealth and experience incorporated for one million dollars the Market Street Cable Railroad. Its equipment was first-class in every respect. The line was in competition with eight other street-car companies, and it immediately became the favorite with the riding public owing to the convenience and comfort of the cars, the speed with which they traveled, and their frequency.

The building of this road had the effect of stimulating real-estate development south of Market and in the Valencia district. All those portions of the city which the lines served immediately felt the influence of rapid transportation. The Valencia (blue-colored), Haight (red-colored), and McAllister (yellow-colored) lines were first operated. The Hayes (green-colored) line was built a year or two later. The Castro (ivory-white-colored) was built in 1887 under the Market Street and Fairmont Railway Company franchise—the route was on Castro Street from Market to Twenty-sixth Street. Since the main lines of the road ran on Market Street, the principal thoroughfare of San Francisco, and several millions were spent on expansion, the Market Street Cable was destined to become the most important street-car system of this city. The defeatists of that period supposed that a cable railroad on the main street would be impracticable, owing to its congested state at certain hours of the day. Many thought the cars would have to move so slowly that they would be unpopular. It was found that the considerable speed maintained by the cars tended to make people more cautious than on slow roads. Teamsters knew that the cars ran fast and, at the first sound of the gong, cleared the tracks. The speed proved highly advantageous and satisfactory to the public.

The Market Street Cable Company promoted baseball and special events and on Saturdays and Sundays carried capacity loads. A steam dummy line was operated by the Park and Ocean Railroad Company from Haight and Stanyan, out H Street (now Lincoln Way), through the Park to Forty-ninth Avenue and in a northerly direction paralleling the beach to the Seal Rock House. The fare on this line was five cents.

Cable Car Days in San Francisco

The Powell Street line, a branch of the Ferries and Cliff House Railroad, was built in 1887 and is still in operation. One of the most attractive features of the city, it is appreciated by visitors. This company was the first to use the lever-bottom grip.

The Omnibus Cable Company succeeded the Omnibus Railroad and Cable Company, whose predecessor was the Omnibus Railroad Company, operating horsecars on Howard Street and on Third and Montgomery streets from the Southern Pacific depot to North Beach, also a branch line down Spear Street to the Oregon and Oceanic Steamship docks, as well as on Brannan Street from Third Street to the Pacific Mail docks.

The new company carried into effect an ambitious program of building a cable road from the ferries along East Street (now the Embarcadero) and out Howard to Twenty-sixth Street, with a branch over Twenty-fourth to Potrero Avenue. From Tenth and Howard, a cable line was built over Tenth, Fell, Franklin, Oak, and Stanyan streets to Haight Street, where its turntable was placed a few feet away from the Haight Street turntable. The Ellis Street line also was operated from this point, leaving the Oak Street line at Broderick, to Ellis, and down Ellis to Market Street, also from Tenth and Howard, over Tenth, Polk, Grove, Park or City Hall Avenue, to Leavenworth, and Post to Market, where connections were made with a new horsecar line on Market from Post to the ferries. The Post Street line was the most difficult cable road ever put in operation, as it had to drop its rope over six intersecting lines and operated around five curves. This caused excessive wear on the cables, which rarely lasted over four months.

While its westbound fares were mostly cash, its eastbound traffic was predominantly on transfers; and while it gave splendid service to the public, it was not very profitable.

When the horsecars were discarded on Howard Street, the company opened a new line with them from Tenth and Howard, over Tenth, Potrero Avenue, and out San Bruno Road to Silver Avenue, with a branch over Oakdale Avenue to Railroad Avenue (now Third Street).

This company inaugurated the first universal-transfer system over its own lines, so that a person could ride from the Bayview district and the Mission to Golden Gate Park, North Beach, the Southern Pacific depot or the ferries, all for one fare, which made it a very popular system. This transfer privilege, however, was abused by the public, who soon found that they could make round trips for a single fare, and that led to the present system of transfers, punched to indicate time and direction.

The cable cars were the most expensive built up to that time, costing $1,900 apiece; and the company gave very good service. The Market Street Railway, with its superior finances, soon began a life-and-death struggle with the new system. Whereas this company had exacted two fares for the trip from the Mission to the Park, it now had to meet the competition by transfers.

The Omnibus Company used a special rail designed by them and made by the Pacific Rolling Mills. It had a flange on each side of the running surface. They thus infringed on patents held by the Johnson Stout Steel Rail Company, and were sued, along with the rolling mills, for two million dollars. The suit was finally compromised by a heavy payment made by the Omnibus Company—the competitors, by the way, subsequently bought a large quantity of rail from the Johnson Company. A unique construction feature was a three-way complicated crossing at Market and Tenth streets—three slots meeting at one point.

Both the Market Street and the Omnibus companies then asked for franchises to extend their respective services. The worst clash came regarding the traffic to the Ocean Beach. The Market Street Railway Company, through a subsidiary, the Park and Ocean Railroad, operated a steam dummy from the Haight Street terminus, out Lincoln Way to Ocean Beach, where the present loop of the No. 5 and No. 7 lines is now in existence. An extra fare was exacted for this ride, and on Sundays there was a very heavy patronage. But with the advent of the Omnibus Company to the common terminus of the Haight Street, the Park and Ocean, and the Omnibus lines, the Omnibus Company took over 50 per cent of the Ocean Beach traffic, much to the discomfiture of the Market Street Railway Company.

The latter now determined to extend its cable line to First Avenue, where the Ocean Beach steam trains would terminate, thus removing them from the vicinity of the Omnibus terminal. The Market Street Company actually constructed its tracks on Stanyan south of Haight, leaving a gap which was to be closed in by removal of the Haight Street turntable and connecting the new track with a curve to the Haight Street line.

The Omnibus Company, biding its time, took advantage of this situation and one very rainy Saturday night brought its construction crews to this terminal, where they built about 110 feet of track, connecting their turntable with the new Stanyan Street tracks. They concreted them solidly and promptly ran cars over the tracks in order to hold them against possible opponents.

These cars were filled with construction crews. Food and beverages, soft and otherwise, were provided, also card tables for the convenience of the crews. The Market Street Company later sent out their own construction crews for the purpose of tearing up these tracks. But the Market Street Company had failed to provide entertainment and re-freshments for their crews, and it is easy to conclude which of the crews remained in possession over the succeeding Sunday.

Of course, this short track connection was of a different gauge, being 3′ 6″, as against the Market Street's standard gauge of 4′ 8½″. However, the maneuver prevented the latter company from putting in its curve, and the Omnibus Company remained in possession of its share of the Ocean Beach business, which was augmented by the ad-jacent baseball grounds and the convenient location of the bandstand in Golden Gate Park, prior to the Mid-Winter Fair.

A further complication in the fight herein described developed when the San Francisco and San Mateo electric line, which also had a franchise on Stanyan Street, became jittery and laid an electric track on top of the Market Street cable tracks. This in turn aroused the Metropolitan line, with the result that one cable track was surmounted by two electric tracks, not one of which could be used. It was a battle royal that attracted crowds on that rainy Sunday, to watch the opera-tions, which included many fights among the workmen of the four companies concerned.

This was probably the last physical battle of the kind, for in 1893 a great consolidation of the cable systems took place. The Market Street Railway Company, throwing in all its subsidiary horsecar lines, secured 76 per cent of the stock in the new Market Street Railway Company, the Omnibus Company, including its majority ownership in the North Beach and Mission Railway Company, received 16 per cent, and the Ferries and Cliff House Railroad received 8 per cent. This was the closing chapter of the cable-car railroad building in San Francisco.

The only cable line constructed after this consolidation was the extension of the Sacramento Street line to Fulton Street, mentioned in the description of the Ferries and Cliff House Railway.

GEO. W. GERHARD

Appendix

STATISTICS ON HORSE AND CABLE RAILROAD OPERATIONS

The following table shows the number of miles (single track) of horse and cable railroads in San Francisco for the years 1872, 1884, and 1888, with the population of the city, the number of passengers carried, and number of times the whole population of the city is carried annually.[1]

Year	Miles of Single Track, Horse	Miles of Single Track, Cable	Population of City	Passengers Carried	Population Carried
1872	70	None	188,000	18,801,574	100 times
1884	60	50.00	215,000	44,635,000	168 times
1888	63	59.44	290,000	67,363,239	232 times

CABLE STATISTICS*

Route	Length in Feet†	Time of Round Trip	Speed		Life (Days)
			Feet per Minute	Miles per Hour	
Kearny Street	13,400	15m 10s	883	10.03	370
California Street...	18,600	19 25	966	10.90	490
Hyde Street	12,500	14 20	872	9.90	240
Jones Street	14,500	17 00	853	9.69	220

* Source: Corporation records, California Street Cable Railroad Company.
† Weight per foot, 2.60 pounds; cost, 13 cents per pound.

It is to be observed that each of the horsecars in the early 'seventies had a speed of 4 miles an hour, carried 24 seated passengers, and operated on a 2½-minute headway. The cable car and dummy traveled at 6 miles per hour, had a capacity of 48 passengers, and operated with a headway of 5 minutes.

By using its full capacity as a horsecar line with a 2½-minute instead of a 5-minute headway, the Market Street Railroad, as it was constituted in 1873, at best could produce a maximum gross income of $475 a day. The actual gross income, however, amounted to only $130,000 per annum or $359 per day. By a change to cable propulsion, with double seating capacity and reduced operating expenses, a vast improvement became available.

[1] Source: *Langley's City Directory*, 1889.

SAN FRANCISCO CABLE RAILROADS*

Name of Road	Beginning of Operation	Length of Road, Double Track (Feet)	Weight of Car and Dummy† (Pounds)	No. of Cars Used‡	Headway (Minutes)	Cable Speed (Feet per Minute)	Status in 1944
Clay Street Hill	Sept. 1, 1873	5,300	4,900	7	3 to 5	528	Motor Coaches
Sutter Street Railroad	Jan. 27, 1877	17,000	5,000	14	4	421	Muni., elec.
California Street Railroad	Apr. 9, 1878	12,600	8,600	14	5	537	Operating
Geary Street Park and Ocean Railroad	Feb. 16, 1880	13,200	8,400	16	5	600	Muni., elec.
Presidio and Ferries Railroad	Oct. 23, 1880	13,000	8,600	15	5	537	Muni., elec.
Market Street Railroad	Aug. 22, 1883	44,200	9,600	36	4	750	Muni., elec.
Ferries and Cliff House Railroad	1888	....	....	....	....	....	Unchanged
Omnibus Cable Company	Aug. 26, 1888	....	....	....	....	....	Muni., elec.

* Source: *Market Street Cable Company.* San Francisco. H. S. Crocker & Co., 1884.

† Each road used a separate dummy car to carry the grip except the Market Street. They built the first combined car eliminating the dummy.

‡ Average in use on weekdays.

HORSE AND CABLE RAILROAD OPERATIONS*

Name of Company and Number of Branches and Main Lines	No. of Tickets for 25 Cents	No. of Men Employed	No. of Horses Used	No. of Cars Used	Total Length (Miles)	Passengers Carried	Gross Earnings
Omnibus (2 main, 1 branch)	5	125	280	30	6½	4,670,000	$ 233,500
North Beach and Mission (2 main)	5	130	250	30	6	4,274,000	213,700
Central (2 main)	4	80	215	22	5	2,670,000	171,600
Sutter Street (1 main, 3 branch)	4	75	180	19	8	1,750,000	113,000
City (Woodward's) (1 main, 1 branch)	5	80	200	26	4	3,500,000	130,000
Market Street (1 main, 1 branch)	5	80	209	23	6	2,787,000	130,000
Potrero and Bayview (1 main)	4	33	58	9	3½	538,000	34,000
Clay Street Hill (1 main)	5	33	22	10	3	No returns	......
Grand totals for 1873	..	636	1,414	..	42	20,189,000	$1,025,800
Grand totals for 1872	..	598	1,391	..	40½	18,801,000	$ 935,812

* Source: *Langley's City Directory,* 1874.

Appendix

It is of further statistical value to list some of the wages paid for labor and prices paid for materials during 1873 and particularly during the Clay Street Hill Cable Railway construction:

Machinists . . . . $ 3.00 per day
Carpenters . . . .   3.00 per day
Hod carriers . . . .   2.00 per day
Laborers . . . .   1.50 per day
Conductors . . . .   2.50 per day
Bricks . . . .   10.00 per one thousand
Cement . . . .   4.00 per three hundred pounds
Rails, iron . . . .   60.00 per ton
Coal . . . .   8.50 per ton

The foregoing data illustrate the advantageous economic possibilities created by the new cable railroad system as compared with the old horsecar transportation.

The resulting profits in the succeeding years confirmed these expectations to a large extent in addition to giving efficient transportation to San Francisco for that period. Nor can it be denied that, as previously pointed out, the city never could have made anywhere near the tremendous and rapid progress shown in that period without the aid of this radical change in its transportation methods.

CONDITIONS UNDER WHICH THE VARIOUS CABLE ROADS OPERATED*

Item	Clay Street Hill Railroad	Sutter Street Railroad	California Street Railroad	Geary Street Railroad
Commenced operating	Sept. 1, 1873	Jan. 27, 1877	Apr. 9, 1878	Feb. 16, 1880
Length of road, double track	5,300 ft.	Sutter St., 13,291 ft., Larkin St., 3,712 ft.	12,651 ft.	13,200 ft.
Heaviest grade	307 ft. in 2,800	167 ft. in 4,300	265 ft. in 2,800	83 ft. in 1,925
Number of engines employed	2	6 (4 on Larkin St., 2 on Cemetery Ave.)	2	2
Dimensions of cylinders	14 x 28 in.	12 x 24 in.	22 x 36 in.	18 x 48 in.
Piston speed per minute	532 ft.	340 ft.	540 ft.	368 ft.
Number of boilers	2	6	3 fire box	3 steel
Diameter and thickness of shell	16 ft. x 54 in. diam., 5/16 in. thick 16 ft. x 48 in. diam., 5/16 in. thick	2 ea. 54 ft. x 16 in. diam., 3/8 in. thick 3 ea. 48 ft. x 16 in. diam., 3/8 in. thick 1 ea. 52 ft. x 16 in. diam., 3/8 in. thick	57 in. diam., 7/16 in. thick	52 in. diam. 16 ft. long, 3/8 in. thick
Number and size of tubes	42 3-inch tubes 56 3½-inch tubes	53 3-inch tubes 53 3-inch tubes 58 3-inch tubes 49 3-inch tubes	81 tubes, 3 in. diam. 12 ft. long	63 tubes, 3 in. diameter, steel
Average pressure in boilers	67½ lbs.	100 lbs.	70 lbs.	65 lbs.
Pressure necessary to move	16 lbs.	40 lbs.	15 lbs.	9 lbs.
Consumption of coal per day, and kind	3,700 lbs. Wallsend, Sydney	24,640 lbs. Seattle Nut Coal	15,680 lbs. Seattle Screenings	11,230 lbs. Seattle Nut
Weight of empty car	2,800 lbs.	3,000 lbs.	4,000 lbs.	4,000 lbs.

Weight of empty dummy	2,100 lbs.	2,000 lbs.	3,000 lbs.	4,800 lbs.
Intervals of departure	3 to 5 min.	4 min. average	5 min. average	2½ to 6 min.
Average number of round trips per day	221	253	226	228
Average number of cars and dummies employed	7 of each	14 of each	14 of each	16 weekdays; 20 Sundays
Hours run per day	17½	19½	19	19
Number of wire ropes in use	1	4 (Sutter St. 3; Larkin St. 1)	2	2
Lengths of rope used	11,000 ft.	11,587 ft. 7,849 ft. 9,800 ft. 8,500 ft.	8,840 and 17,055 ft.	16,600 and 11,000 ft.
Circumference of wire rope	3 1/16 in.	3 in.	4½ and 4 in.	3 in.
Kind of ropes used	Crucible steel, 6 strands of 19 wires	Crucible steel, 6 strands of 19 wires	Crucible steel, 6 strands of 19 wires, Norway iron	Crucible steel, 6 strands of 19 wires
Speed at which ropes travel	528 ft. per min.	430 ft. and 786 ft per min.	537 ft. per min.	600 and 650 ft. per min.
Average life of ropes	547 days	304 days	373 days	274 days
Remarks	The engine house is located on top of the hill and about midway between the two ends.	This company has two engine houses. In one there are 4 engines and in the other are 2.	The engine house of this company is located in the hollow, 4,220 ft. from Kearny St.	The engine house of this company is located 8,000 ft. from Kearny St.

* Source: *Mining and Scientific Press*, September 3, 1881.

REFERENCES

ARNOLD, BION J., *Report on the Improvement and Development of the Transportation Facilities of San Francisco,* 1913.

BAILEY, MILLARD, "History of San Francisco Bay Regions," *The American Historical Society, Inc.,* III (1924), 312.

BANCROFT, HUBERT R., *History of California,* VII (1890).

City Directory of San Francisco of 1878, "Street Railways."

CROSS, IRA D., *Financing the Empire, History of Banking in California,* 1927.

Daggett's Scrap Book (in State Library at Sacramento), 1, 2. (No note as to the source of the newspaper clipping April 26, 1900, on A. S. Hallidie.)

HALLIDIE, ANDREW SMITH, *A. S. Hallidie's System of Cable Railroads,* San Francisco, 1880.

——, *A. S. Hallidie's Wire Rope Traction Street Railway,* San Francisco, 1875.

——, "A Brief History of the Cable Railway System, Its Origin and Progress, and Papers in Connection Therewith," *Report of the Mechanics' Institute Exposition [1890],* San Francisco, P. J. Thomas, Printer, 1891.

——, *The Invention of the Cable Railway System,* San Francisco, 1885.

——, *Mr. A. S. Hallidie's Patent System of Wire-Rope Traction Street Tramway.* Printed by J. Moore, Scientific Press, 1876.

——, *A Biographical Sketch of Andrew Smith Hallidie,* New York, 1897.

HARDY, LADY DUFFUS, *Through City and Prairie Lands,* Chapman & Hall, 1881.

HARPENDING, ASBURY, *The Great Diamond Hoax.* Edited by J. H. Wilkins, 1913.

IRWIN, WILL, *Pictures of Old Chinatown,* Moffatt Yard, New York, 1908.

LLOYD, B. E., *Light and Shades of San Francisco,* A. L. Bancroft & Co., 1876.

MARYE, G. T., JR., *From '49 to '83 in California and Nevada,* San Francisco, 1923.

NEVILLE, AMELIA, *The Fantastic City,* Houghton Mifflin Co., Boston, 1932.

PUBLIC.WORKS, DEPARTMENT OF, BUREAU OF ENGINEERING, *The Municipal Railway of San Francisco, 1912–1921.*

ROOT, HENRY, *Personal History and Reminiscences, 1845–1921.* Privately printed.

RUSSELL, HUBERT D., *Complete Story of the San Francisco Horror,* San Francisco, 1906.

SAN FRANCISCO, SUPERVISORS, BOARD OF, *San Francisco Municipal Reports for the Fiscal Years 1869–1870, 1870–71, etc., to 1899.*

STETSON, JAMES B., *San Francisco During the Eventful Days of 1906.* Privately printed.

TODD, FRANK MORTON, *A Romance of Insurance* (for the Fireman's Fund Insurance Company), H. S. Crocker & Co., 1929.

WILLIAMS, SAMUEL, *City of the Golden Gate, 1875,* Book Club of California.

YOUNG, JOHN P., *San Francisco,* 2 vols., S. J. Clarke Publishing Co.

The biographical material on the Hallidie chapter was obtained from manuscripts and printed articles (mostly by Hallidie himself) which comprise the Hallidie Papers in the Library of the California Historical Society in San Francisco.